D1233305

BOMBERS AND RECONNAISSANCE AIRCRAFT

WAR PLANES OF THE SECOND WORLD WAR

BOMBERS
AND RECONNAISSANCE AIRCRAFT

VOLUME NINE

WILLIAM GREEN

With Drawings by Dennis I. Punnett

MACDONALD : LONDON

Third impression March 1970

© William Green, 1968

SBN 356 01491 6

First published in 1968 by
Macdonald & Co. (Publishers) Ltd.
49/50 Poland Street, London, W.1
Made and printed in Great Britain by
Purnell & Sons, Ltd.
Paulton (Somerset) and London

INTRODUCTION

It was the fond boast of *Reichsmarschall* Hermann Göring that in 1933 Germany had not possessed a single modern fighter or bomber, yet, within the space of six short years, he had created in the *Luftwaffe* the world's most powerful and modern air arm. This claim was not entirely accurate as the clandestine *Fliegerstab* of the *Reichswehr* had been planning since the late 'twenties for the day when German rearmament would become a fact, and much of the small but energetic German aircraft industry had begun the design and construction of combat aircraft before the birth of the Third Reich. However, the forging of so potent an air striking weapon was none the less remarkable for the fact that its foundations had been prepared by the *Reichswehr* before Göring was entrusted with the evolution of the *Luftwaffe*.

Equally remarkable was the rapidity of the parallel growth of the German aircraft industry; the speed with which it absorbed the latest technological advances, and the exceptional creative capabilities evinced by its warplane designers, which, in certain spheres, placed Germany ahead of the world. One such sphere was that of tactical bomber development. The bombers of the *Luftwaffe* were, as was to be expected, vaunted by German propagandists of the period and derided by their Allied opposite numbers, but with the passage of time and the availability of authentic records buried in archives for nearly a quarter-century, it is possible to place their shortcomings and successes in perspective.

One bomber, the Heinkel He 111, the development and career of which is exhaustively described in this volume, which continues the coverage of German bombers and reconnaissance aircraft initiated by Volume Eight, was frequently belittled. Its

début in the mid 'thirties in the guise of a commercial transport with, it was subsequently to be claimed, few concessions to its ostensibly more pacific role to gain its acceptance by a gullible aeronautical community, has often been instanced as a glaring example of German duplicity and subterfuge. In fact, the He 111 transport was not a derivative of the bomber, nor the bomber a derivative of the transport, both being parallel developments of the one basic design evolved to a specification framed by the *Reichsluftfahrtministerium* and *Deutsche Lufthansa* in close collaboration. Both required a high-speed twin-engined aircraft embodying state-of-the-art structural and aerodynamic techniques, the former for use as a medium bomber by the still clandestine *Luftwaffe* and the latter as a 10-passenger prestige-building airliner. The differing demands of the two roles were by no means incompatible at this time, as, from the DLH viewpoint, operating economics were a secondary consideration. The result was an airliner that gained international prestige both for Germany's national airline and for her fledgeling aircraft industry, and a bomber which, during the opening phases of the war, provided the *Luftwaffe* with a formidable offensive weapon; an elegant, well-built and efficient aircraft with good flying characteristics and a respectable performance.

The development of the strategic bomber in Germany was fraught with greater difficulties than was the tactical bomber. The *Luftwaffe*'s first Chief-of-Staff, Lieut.-Gen. Wever, was an ardent protagonist of the long-range strategic bomber and, as early as 1935, had initiated the so-called "Ural Bomber" programme, but with Wever's death in June 1936, his successor, Gen. Albert Kesselring, concluded that the primary role of the *Luftwaffe* should remain tactical; that the "Ural Bomber" concept was years ahead of the contemporary political situation and, in some respects, the state-of-the-art insofar as the German aircraft industry was concerned. Thus, development of the heavy strategic bomber stagnated in Germany until 1938, when, somewhat belatedly, the design of the He 177 was begun. As recorded in this volume, the development of the *Greif*, as the He 177 was dubbed, was to provide the most dismal chapter in the wartime record of the German aircraft industry.

The lack of a long-range aircraft such as the He 177 suitable for use as a commerce raider did, however, result in one of the most remarkable and successful examples of improvisation in the history of military aviation —the Focke-Wulf Fw 200C Condor. Having little more than a good endurance to commend it, the Condor, nevertheless, demanded an inordinate effort on the part of the Allies before its threat was finally nullified, and was to be referred to by the late Sir Winston Churchill as the scourge of the Atlantic.

As much a failure as the Condor was a success was Germany's "Bomber B" programme which called for an extremely advanced high-altitude bomber to succeed the He 111 and Ju 88. Intended to carry medium bomber design a significant step forward, the "Bomber B" programme staggered on for four years, resulting in such types as the Do 317 and the Fw 191 to be found in the pages that follow, but none of its progeny was destined to achieve operational service.

The contents of this volume range from what was considered by World War II standards to be the ultra modern, as represented by the previously-mentioned "Bomber B" programme prototypes, to such types as the Heinkel He 46 and Henschel Hs 123 which were considered obsolescent when the *Luftwaffe* went to war yet still soldiered on into its closing phases, the coverage of German bombers and reconnaissance aircraft being completed by Volume Ten which describes and illustrates the remaining products in these categories of the Henschel concern, and those of Junkers and Messerschmitt.

In conclusion, I should like to record my thanks to Hans Redemann and Luis de Azaola who have supplied several of the photographs appearing in this volume, and to the Bundesarchiv, Coblenz which has furnished the photographs appearing on pages, 21, 27, 35, 114, 119, 121 (top), and 131.

London, October 1967   William Green

DORNIER DO 215

The international interest aroused in the Do 17 in July 1937 by its success at Zürich was renewed in the following year by the début of the improved Do 17Z, and at an early stage in the development of the new model the Yugoslav government began to consider its capabilities as a potential production successor to the earlier Do 17K for which the *Državna Fabrika Aviona*, or State Aircraft Factory, was in process of tooling. Dornier therefore obtained

(Right and below) The Do 215 V1, a re-engined Do 17Z-0 airframe

7

The Do 215*B-03, the third pre-production aircraft originally built against a Swedish contract and delivered to the Luftwaffe early in* 1940

permission to solicit export orders for the Do 17Z, and although the model to be offered on the export market was, to all intents and purposes, identical to that being manufactured for the *Luftwaffe*, apart from equipment, the *Reichsluftfahrtministerium* (RLM) insisted on allocating a new type designation to the aircraft in export form.

A pre-production Do 17Z-0 was given the civil registration D-AIIB and, duly redesignated **Do 215 V1**, served as a demonstration aircraft. In view of the interest displayed by Yugoslavia, a second Do 17Z-0 airframe was re-engined with a pair of Gnôme-Rhône 14 N 1/2 14-cylinder air-cooled radials in place of the Bramo Fafnir 323A-1 nine-cylinder radials as the **Do 215 V2** and demonstrated to the Royal Yugoslav Air Force. However, the Do 215 V2 did not offer a sufficient performance advance over the Do 17K already in production in Yugoslavia, and therefore a third airframe was allocated to the Do 215 development programme, and this, the **Do 215 V3**, was powered by two Daimler-Benz DB 601A 12-cylinder liquid-cooled engines each rated at 1,075 h.p. for take-off. Demonstrated during the late spring of 1939, the Do 215 V3 offered a noteworthy improvement in performance.

The Do 215 V3 was demonstrated to several foreign missions and, in the autumn of 1939, after the French government had cancelled the Swedish contract for the Breguet 694, the Swedish government placed an order with Dornier for 18 **Do 215A-1** bombers, these being essentially similar to the Do 215 V3 and carrying a crew of four and a 2,205-lb. bomb load. Production of the Do 215A-1 against the Swedish contract began late in 1939, but before the first delivery could be effected an embargo was placed on the export of the bomber which was adapted on the production line for long-range reconnaissance tasks with the *Luftwaffe* as the **Do 215B-0** and **B-1**. These aircraft reached the *Luftwaffe* in January-February 1940, and were promptly issued to 3.Aufkl.St./ Ob.d.L., one of the *Staffeln* of the reconnais-

8

sance *Gruppe* attached to the *Oberbefehlshaber der Luftwaffe*, the *Luftwaffe* High Command. This unit was operating from Stavanger, Norway, shortly after the airfield's capture in April 1940, with 13 Do 215B-0 and B-1 aircraft and three He 111s on strength.

By this time, Dornier had been ordered to continue Do 215 production for the *Luftwaffe*, and in March 1940 began delivery of the **Do 215B-4** which differed from the B-1 in its camera equipment, an Rb 50/30 camera being mounted beneath the lower gun position and an Rb 20/30 camera being installed in the crew entry hatch. For combined bombing and reconnaissance missions five 110-lb. bombs were normally carried, but up to 10 110-lb. bombs could be carried on short-range missions, and for long-range and ferry missions the two 170.5 Imp. gal. standard fuel tanks in the wings between the fuselage and engine nacelles could be aug-mented by a 197 Imp. gal. auxiliary tank in the bomb-bay. Defen-sive armament com-prised two forward-firing 7.9-mm. MG 15 machine guns, two similar weapons firing to port and starboard from the rear of the cockpit, and a further pair of MG 15s firing aft from above and below the fuselage. The designation **Do 215B-2** had been allocated to a pure bomber variant that was not proceeded with, while **Do 215B-3** was the designation applied to the two ex-amples supplied early

(Above and below) A Do 215B-1 (NO-TB) under test prior to delivery to the Aufkl.Gr./Ob.d.L.

in 1940 to the Soviet Union under the Russo-German Agreement.

By May 1940, all three *Staffeln* of the Aufkl. Gr./Ob.d.L. had Do 215Bs on strength, 1. *Staffel* operating three Do 215Bs, two Bf 110Ds and seven He 111s, and 2. and 3. *Staffel* both being completely Do 215B-equipped with 10 and 11 aircraft respectively. In the meantime, limited production of the Do 215B was continued by Dornier until the beginning of 1941 when the 101st and last example left the assembly line. At that time, the only *Luftwaffe* unit operating the Do 215B was still the Aufkl. Gr./Ob.d.L., and the 1. *Staffel* was operating a mixture of Do 215B-4s and Do 217A-0s on long-range reconnaissance sorties, and 2. and 3. *Staffel* were employing Do 215B-4s in concert with other types, such as the Ju 88A. Earlier, nine Do 17Z bomber airframes had been converted as night intruders under the designation Do 17Z-10 Kauz II (Screech Owl II), and at the end of 1940 the Ju 88C-2-equipped *Nachtjagdgruppe* 2 formed a fourth *Staffel* on this type at Gilze-Rijen in the Netherlands for nocturnal sorties against R.A.F. bomber bases in East Anglia, Lincolnshire and Yorkshire. Offering a generally superior performance to that of the Do 17Z, early in 1941 it was decided to convert a dozen Do 215B airframes for night intruder tasks. A special nose section had been designed for the Do 17Z-10, this housing four 7.9-mm. MG 17 machine guns and two 20-mm. MG FF cannon, and this was applied to the Do 215B which thus became the **Do 215B-5**. These aircraft were delivered to 4./NJG 2 in the spring and early summer of 1941, continuing nocturnal sorties over Britain until the unit was transferred to Sicily in the following October.

Early in 1942, a number of the *Luftwaffe*'s Do 215B-4s were transferred to the Hungarian Air Force, replacing the Heinkel He 111H and with the I Long-Range Reconnaissance Group subsequently operating on the Russian Front until supplanted by the Junkers Ju 88. In *Luftwaffe* service, the Do 215B had virtually disappeared from first-line service by 1942, and surviving examples were mostly relegated to various test roles.

The definitive production version of the Do 215, the B-4, the 40th example of which is illustrated below, had an Rb 50/30 camera below the lower gun

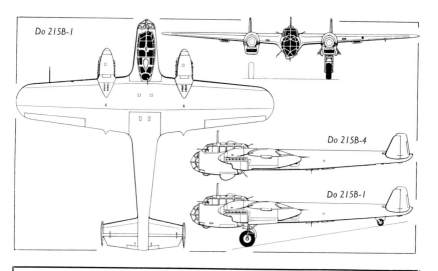

Do 215B-1

Do 215B-4

Do 215B-1

DORNIER DO 215B-1 SPECIFICATION

Type: *Four-seat Medium Reconnaissance-Bomber.* **Power Plants:** *Two Daimler-Benz DB 601Aa 12-cylinder liquid-cooled engines each rated at 1,100 h.p. for take-off.* **Armament:** *Two forward-firing 7.9-mm. MG 15 (either fixed or free-mounted), two free-mounted 7.9-mm. MG 15 machine guns firing to port and starboard, and two aft firing free-mounted 7.9-mm. MG 15 machine guns, one above and one below the fuselage. (Offensive) Maximum internal bomb load of 2,205 lb., typical loads including 20 110-lb. SD 50 or four 551-lb. SD 250 bombs.* **Performance:** *Maximum speed, 239 m.p.h. at sea level, 289 m.p.h. at 13,120 ft., 292 m.p.h. at 16,400 ft.; maximum cruising speed, 255 m.p.h. at 13,120 ft.; tactical radius (with standard fuel and 2,205-lb. bomb load), 236 mls.; maximum range (with 192 Imp. gal. auxiliary bomb-bay tank), 1,520 mls.; initial climb rate, 1,195 ft./min.; service ceiling, 29,530 ft.* **Weights:** *Empty equipped, 12,730 lb.; maximum loaded, 19,400 lb.* **Dimensions:** *Span, 59 ft. 0⅛ in.; length, 51 ft. 9⅞ in.; height, 14 ft. 11½ in.; wing area, 592.014 sq. ft.*

The success achieved by the Do 17 series of bombers and reconnaissance aircraft led, in 1937, to a proposal on the part of the Dornier-Werke for a scaled-up development of the basic design to meet a requirement formulated by the *Technische Amt* of the *Reichsluftfahrt-ministerium* (RLM) calling for a longer-ranging, heavier and more versatile warplane,

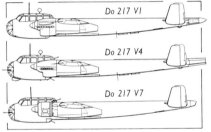

capable of lifting substantially larger offensive loads and delivering these in level or diving attack.

Classified as a heavy bomber, the project received the designation Do 217. Prototypes were ordered in the early summer of 1937 and, from the outset of design work, the structure of the new warplane was arranged to offer maximum suitability for mass production, and to take air-cooled and liquid-cooled engines with equal facility. It followed generally the lines established by the Do 17 models then under development with deepened forward fuselages, but apart from this strong external family resemblance the Do 217 bore little relationship to its predecessor, being both structurally and aerodynamically an entirely new aircraft.

Retaining the shoulder-mounted wing arrangement, the Do 217 featured an all-metal two-spar wing, all but a few former ribs of which were girder trusses with solid plate ribs being employed at points of stress. The outer

The third Jumo-powered prototype, the Do 217 V4, joined the test programme early in 1939, and was the first aircraft in the series with armament

portion of each wing was attached to the centre section by means of four large bolts at each spar and a score of smaller bolts through flanges around the periphery of the wing section between the spars, the whole being covered by a riveted stressed skin. Slotted ailerons were carried by the outer sections, these being linked with electrically-operated split flaps on the inboard section.

The structural design of the fuselage differed to a more marked degree from earlier Dornier practice. An all-metal structure built in three sections of which the centre portion was integral with the wing centre section, the fuselage comprised continuous rolled Z-section stringers passing through cut-outs in the frames, and at the top, bottom and lower sides of the fuselage these gave place to members of extruded T-section. Each fuselage section was joined to the next by 25 bolts

passing through flanges riveted to the skin. Crew accommodation followed what was by now becoming standard German practice for bombers in that all four members were grouped together ahead of the wing leading edge, with pilot seated to port and bombardier to starboard, the radio-operator behind the pilot, and the gunner, who was intended to operate the lower aft-firing free-mounted weapon, between the bombardier and the radio-operator.

One of the most novel features of the Do 217's design was the dive brake which was attached to the extreme rear fuselage. This brake operated somewhat after the fashion of a parachute, or a four-ribbed umbrella, the "ribs" when closed forming the four sides of the tail extension. The brake was operated by a threaded collar and spindle, the movement of the collar pulling the "ribs" open against four short hinged struts. This air brake had been

tested exhaustively by a Do 17M-1, and the trials had given promising results.

Powered by two Daimler-Benz DB 601A 12-cylinder liquid-cooled engines each rated at 1,075 h.p. for take-off, the first prototype, the **Do 217 V1**, was flown for the first time in August 1938, but it was immediately apparent that despite its external similarity to the Do 17, the new bomber did not emulate entirely the good-natured flying characteristics of its predecessor. There was a marked tendency to swing during take-off, directional stability left much to be desired, and control response was sluggish, and in September the aircraft crashed and was totally destroyed while engaged in single-engined low-altitude trials near Tettnang im Allgäu, Dornier's test pilot, Koeppe, and the accompanying mechanic losing their lives.

Before the end of 1938, the second and third prototypes, the **Do 217 V2** and **V3**, had been completed, these being essentially similar to the first prototype apart from having Junkers Jumo 211A 12-cylinder liquid-cooled engines rated at 950 h.p. for take-off. The two prototypes continued the flight development programme, one being largely concerned with diving trials during which it was discovered that, while the tail brake functioned relatively efficiently on the Do 17M-1 test-bed, it was not so satisfactory on the larger and more heavily loaded Do 217. The brake proved unreliable in operation and exerted severe strain on the rear fuselage, resulting in the distortion of stringers and the buckling of the stressed skin. Early in 1939, a third Jumo-engined prototype, the **Do 217 V4** (D-AMSD), joined the test programme, this being intended as the production prototype and was the first aircraft of the series to carry armament, a single free-mounted 7.9-mm. MG 15 protruding through the starboard side of the nose glazing and similar aft-firing weapons being mounted above and below the fuselage. The Do 217 V4 also embodied a long dorsal strake as an attempt to rectify the stability problem, a redesigned tail brake, enlarged rudder trim tabs and other minor changes, and was delivered to the *Erprobungsstelle* at Rechlin for official evaluation. In general, the Rechlin test pilot's reports were unfavourable, stability being poor and performance falling short of requirements. The *Technische Amt* considered that the Do 217 V4 made inadequate provision for new systems and equipment then under development, and with fuel for extended-range operations insufficient space was available for large-calibre bombs, torpedoes or mines.

While the RLM evaluation was proceeding, Dornier was building further prototypes and was initiating construction of a batch of pre-production aircraft, and the next prototype to fly was a replacement for the original Do 217 V1 and was accordingly designated **Do 217 V1E** (the "E" suffix letter indicating *Ersatz* or Replacement). The Do 217 V1E substituted rods and pulleys for the cable-type control runs of its predecessors, and fixed slots were attached to the leading edges of the tail fins, these effectively improving stability. The **Do 217 V5** and **V6** were similar to the V1E and were tested throughout the summer months of 1939, the latter with various underwing loads, such as 198 Imp. gal. auxiliary fuel tanks. The programme was frequently interrupted by mechanical failures, and as a result of the phenomenally high effective wing loading of the aircraft by standards then appertaining of 63.2 lb. per sq. ft.—the net wing area being 522 sq. ft.—the test pilots continually compared the manoeuvrability of the Do 217 with that of other contemporary aircraft in un-

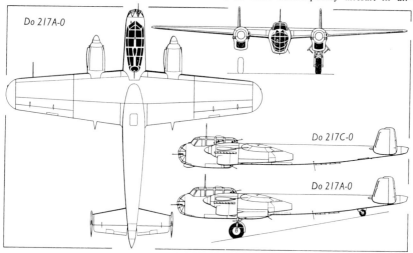

Do 217A-0

Do 217C-0

Do 217A-0

(Above) The sixth pre-production Do 217E-0 (Werk-Nr. 08 00 006) employed by BMW for engine development, and (below) the 12th Do 217E-0 (Werk-Nr. 08 00 012)

mounted air brake and, finally, the *Technische Amt* agreed to the temporary waiving of the dive bombing requirement, permitting Dornier to concentrate on developing the Do 217 for the level bombing and armed anti-shipping reconnaissance tasks, although it was stated categorically that work on perfecting a suitable dive brake had to continue, and this would be incorporated in the bomber as soon as perfected. Prior to this decision being taken, Dornier had begun to look further afield for power plants

favourable terms. Little further success had attended protracted trials with the tail-for the Do 217 as it had become obvious that the bomber would never attain the specified performance with either the DB 601A or the Jumo 211A. Early in 1939, BMW was engaged in the development of a compact, small-diameter, high-performance 14-cylinder radial air-cooled engine, the BMW 139 offering 1,550 h.p. for take-off, and Dornier elected to power the next two prototypes of its heavy bomber, the **Do 217 V7** (D-ACBF) and **V8** (D-AHJE), with the new radial which was enclosed by a long-chord cowling and featured a fan geared to airscrew speed and rotating in the same direction. Neither BMW 139-engined prototypes featured the tail brake extension, and in the event, by the time these aircraft commenced flight trials in the late autumn of 1939, a decision had already been taken to abandon the BMW 139 in favour of the potentially more powerful BMW 801. The additional power promised by the new engine enabled the Dornier team to initiate the redesign of the fuselage of the bomber to accommodate substantially larger and heavier internal loads, and thus overcome one of the RLM's principal objections to the Do 217.

In the meantime, Dornier was engaged in completing a pre-production batch of eight **Do 217A-0** long-range reconnaissance aircraft and four **Do 217C-0** bombers powered by the Daimler-Benz DB 601A. These were, in fact, preceded by a Jumo 211A-engined bomber prototype, the **Do 217C V1** (CN-HL). The Do 217A-0 differed from the prototypes primarily in having the bulged lower contour of the forward fuselage extended aft to provide accommodation for two downward-facing cameras. Defensive armament remained a trio of free-mounted 7.9-mm. MG 15 machine guns, and the eight aircraft were delivered to the *Aufklärungsgruppe/Oberbefehlshaber der Luftwaffe*, the special long-range reconnaissance *Gruppe* commanded by Theodor Rowehl and

(*Above*) *A Do 217E-1 of 5./KG 40 at Bordeaux-Merignac for anti-shipping operations in 1941*

attached to the High Command, during the early spring of 1940. In the early winter of 1940/41, the Do 217A-0s in concert with other aircraft operated by 1. and 3.Aufkl.St./Ob.d.L. flew clandestine photographic missions over Russian territory in preparation for the German attack on the Soviet Union.

The Do 217C-0 bomber was generally similar to the Do 217A-0 reconnaissance aircraft evolved in parallel, but the lower contour of the fuselage reverted to that of the prototypes, provision was made for a 6,614-lb. offensive load, and defensive armament was increased by the introduction of two gimbal-mounted 7.9-mm. MG 15 machine guns firing laterally through the rear upper side windows

(*Above and left*) *An early production Do 217E-2, the first version to feature an electrically operated dorsal turret*

and operated by the wireless operator. In addition, a 15-mm. MG 151 cannon was mounted in the lower port side of the nose and fired by the pilot using a Revi 120 gun sight. As all effort was concentrated on the markedly improved Do 217E by the spring of 1940, no further examples of the Do 217C were manufactured, and the **Do 217C V1** and four pre-production Do 217C-0 aircraft were relegated to the role of equipment and armament test-beds.

DORNIER DO 217E

During the first weeks of 1940, a radically modified prototype, the **Do 217 V9**, was undergoing its initial trials, this, powered by two BMW 801MA 14-cylinder two-row radials each rated at 1,580 h.p. for take-off, being the prototype for the **Do 217E**. The principal change introduced by the Do 217 V9 was a substantial deepening of the fuselage throughout its length. The centre and rear fuselage were divided on the horizontal plane to within a short distance of the tail, the lower half of the fuselage forming the bomb-bay and the remainder containing transverse bracing frames to support the weight of the bomb load, a fuel tank and dinghy stowage. The bomb-bay itself was 14 ft. 10 in. in length, and a 5 ft. 8 in. extension was provided to enable a torpedo to be accommodated, the whole being enclosed by three sets of doors. The BMW 801MA engines drove three-bladed Schwarz airscrews of wooden construction and were supplied as "power eggs", their mountings attaching by four ball-and-socket joints to the forward spar, and all services were electrically actuated, including undercarriage retraction and bomb-bay door operation.

Preparations for quantity production continued throughout the early months of 1940, and the first pre-production **Do 217E-0**

bombers left the assembly line in the autumn, followed by the first production Do 217E-1s before the end of the year. Essentially similar to the V9, the Do 217E-1 was intended for level bombing and anti-shipping tasks, and was not fitted with the tail dive brake. The bomb-bay provided accommodation for eight 551-lb., four 1,102-lb. or two 2,205-lb. bombs. For strafing a single 15-mm. MG 151 cannon was mounted in the lower port side of the forward fuselage with 250 rounds which were fired by

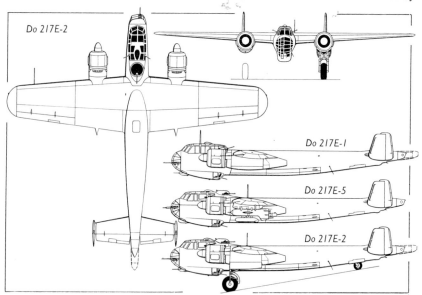

Do 217E-2

Do 217E-1

Do 217E-5

Do 217E-2

The Do 217E-4 (above Werk-Nr. 4381 and below Werk-Nr. 4340) with BMW 801C engines began to appear in operational service early in 1942

the pilot, and defensive armament comprised five 7.9-mm. MG 15 machine guns on gimbal mountings.

With cameras inserted in the bomb-bay, 10 Do 217E-0 and E-1 aircraft were delivered to 2.(F)/11 late in 1940, this *Staffel* being transferred to Rumania in January 1941 to participate in the clandestine photographic reconnaissance of the Soviet Union's periphery, but

Kampfgeschwader 40 was the first unit to take the Do 217E-1 into action, II/KG 40 forming on the type in March 1941 for anti-shipping operations under the command of the *Flieger-führer Atlantik*.

Although the Do 217E-1 proved relatively effective during early operations, experience dictated increases in both offensive and defensive armament, the provision of some armour

protection for the crew, and other changes aimed at increasing the versatility of the basic aircraft. These modifications led to a change in designation to **Do 217E-3**. A free-mounted 20-mm. MG FF cannon was installed in the lower starboard side of the nose for use in anti-shipping strikes, and two additional gimbal-mounted 7.9-mm. MG 15 machine guns were added to fire laterally from cockpit windows immediately aft of the pilot. The Do 217E-3 thus had an imposing array of no fewer than seven 7.9-mm. weapons but, in fact, only a comparatively light weight of fire could be brought to bear as *five* of the guns were intended to be fired by the radio-operator alone. Nevertheless, a wide field of fire was covered. Protection for the crew was provided by 5-mm. and 8.5-mm. plates on the rear cockpit cover, on the top of the fuselage immediately aft of the cockpit and beneath the lower gunner's position. The pilot's seat was armoured, and side plates were added at the lateral-firing gun positions. The versatility of the aircraft was substantially increased by the development of a series of standard *Rüstsätze* (equipment or armament sets) which were, for the most part, applicable to the Do 217E-3 and to other variants of the basic design. The most important of these *Rüstsätze* were as follows:

A Do 217E-4 of III/KG 2 at Gilze-Rijen, Holland, in 1942. The Do 217E-4 differed from the E-2 primarily in having BMW 801C engines

R1 Special 1800 bomb carrier for a single 3,968-lb. SC 1800 bomb with annular fin (applicable to Do 217E-2 and E-3).

R2 Two external racks under outer panels for a pair of 551-lb. SC 250 bombs (applicable to Do 217E-2 and E-3).

R4 PVC 1006 carrier for single L5 torpedo (applicable to Do 217E-1, E-2, E-3, E-4 and K-1).

R5 One 30-mm. MK 101 cannon in lower port side of forward fuselage (applicable to Do 217E-2 and E-3).

R6 Bomb-bay camera installation Do 217E-1, E-2, E-4, K-1 and M-1).

R7 Four-man dinghy pack for installation

DORNIER DO 217E-2 SPECIFICATION

Type: *Four-seat Heavy Bomber.* **Power Plants:** *Two BMW 801ML 14-cylinder two-row radial air-cooled engines each rated at 1,580 h.p. for take-off and 1,380 h.p. at 15,100 ft.* **Armament:** *One fixed forward-firing 15-mm. MG 151 cannon in lower port side of nose, one 13-mm. MG 131 machine gun with 500 rounds in electrically-operated dorsal turret, one free-mounted 13-mm. MG 131 machine gun in ventral step with 1,000 rounds, one free-mounted forward-firing 7.9-mm. MG 15 machine gun and two lateral-firing free-mounted 7.9-mm. MG 15 machine guns, plus (Do 217E-2/R19) four remotely-controlled aft-firing 7.9-mm. MG 81 machine guns in tail cone. (Offensive) Maximum bomb load of 8,818 lb. (5,550 lb. internally). Typical internal loads include eight 551-lb., four 1,102-lb. or two 2,205-lb. plus two 551-lb. bombs.* **Performance:** *Maximum speed, 273 m.p.h. at sea level, 320 m.p.h. at 17,060 ft.; cruising speed (with maximum internal bomb load), 258 m.p.h. at 17,060 ft.; economical cruising speed, 245 m.p.h.; maximum range on standard internal fuel, 1,430 mls., with auxiliary fuel, 1,740 mls.; initial climb rate (with maximum internal bomb load), 710 ft./min.; service ceiling (with maximum internal bomb load), 24,600 ft., (without bomb load), 29,530 ft.* **Weights:** *Empty, 19,522 lb. empty equipped, 23,225 lb.; normal loaded, 33,070 lb.; maximum overload, 36,299 lb.* **Dimensions:** *Span, 62 ft. 4 in.; length, 59 ft. 8½ in.; height, 16 ft. 6 in.; wing area, 613.542 sq. ft.*

A Do 217E-4/R19 of 9./KG 2 with remotely-controlled paired 7.9-mm MG 81 machine guns mounted in the tail cone

22

above bomb-bay, aft of wings (Do 217E-1, E-2, E-4 and K-1).

R8 Auxiliary 165 Imp. gal. fuel tank for installation in forward bomb-bay (applicable to Do 217E-1).

R9 Auxiliary 165 Imp. gal. fuel tank for installation in aft bomb-bay (applicable to Do 217E-1).

R10 Two ETC 2000/XII carriers for Hs 293 stand-off weapons under outer wing panels (applicable to Do 217E-2, E-4 and K-1).

R13 Alternative auxiliary fuel tank of unspecified capacity in forward bomb-bay (applicable to Do 217E-2, E-4, and K-1).

R14 Alternative auxiliary fuel tank of unspecified capacity in aft bomb-bay (applicable to Do 217E-2, E-4 and K-1).

R15 Two ETC 2000/XII carriers for Hs 293 stand-off weapon under wing centre section between fuselage and engine nacelles (applicable to Do 217E-4 and K-2).

R17 One auxiliary 255 Imp. gal. fuel tank for installation in forward bomb-bay (applicable to Do 217E-4 and K-2).

R19 One MG 81Z (paired 7.9-mm. MG 81 machine guns) mounted in tail cone (applicable to Do 217E-2, E-4, K-1, K-2, M-1 and M-11).

R21 Jettison device for external auxiliary fuel tanks (applicable to Do 217E-3, E-4 and

Do 217K-1).

R25 Perlon tail braking chute (applicable to Do 217E-4, K-1, K-2, M-1, M-11 and P).

Despite teething troubles with the tail-mounted dive brake, the RLM was still determined that dive bombing should be added to the repertoire of the Do 217, and in October 1940, prior to the appearance of the Do 217E-3, a pre-production example of a further variant of the bomber, the **Do 217E-2**, had commenced flight trials, this being intended primarily for the dive-bombing role. In fact, although not fitted with the dive brake, the torsion rod extending from the cockpit to the tail of the fuselage to which the screw jack operating the dive brake was attached had been retained by the Do 217E-1 for some inexplicable reason (and was subsequently to be retained by the Do 217E-3). As fitted to the Do 217E-2, the dive brake embodied some improvements, but the most important modification was the introduction of an electrically-operated dorsal turret housing a single 13-mm. MG 131 machine gun with 500 rounds, this effectively improving defensive capability. Simultaneously, the small calibre MG 15 in the ventral step was replaced by an MG 131 with 1,000 rounds. Two 7.9-mm. MG 15s fired laterally from the cockpit, a similar weapon for the bombardier was provided in the extreme nose, and the fixed forward-firing 15-mm. MG 151 cannon was re-

23

The first and second pre-production K-series aircraft, the Do 217K-01 (above) and Do 217K-02 (below), which introduced a redesigned forward fuselage

tained. Power was supplied by two BMW 801ML radials which possessed similar ratings to the BMW 801MA engines of the Do 217E-1 and differed only in the type of airscrew control fitted, the wooden Schwarz-type blades on the VDM hub being supplanted by metal blades, airscrew diameter being increased from 12 ft. 5½ in. to 12 ft. 9½ in.

The RLM gave high priority to the introduction of the Do 217E-2 on the Dornier assembly line, and by the spring of 1941 production of this model was running in parallel with that of the Do 217E-1. A small number of early production Do 217E-2s were issued to Stab/St.G.2, part of a Ju 87-equipped *Geschwader*, for operational evaluation during the early summer of 1941, but results proved unfavourable. Although the operating mechanism of the dive brake was now efficient, the rear fuselage still suffered severe strain and sometimes structural distortion during a dive in which the brake was fully extended, and on occasions the torsion rod actuating the brake was itself distorted, the brake being jammed open after the aircraft had pulled out of the dive, and having to be jettisoned. However, because of its preoccupation with the concept

24

of dive-bombing, and the accuracy of delivery against pin-point targets that it offered, the *Technische Amt* chose to ignore the lack of success that attended evaluation trials.

In an attempt to overcome the problem, during the summer of 1941, Dornier fitted the 36th production Do 217E-2 with new dive brakes which took the form of slotted plates which, mounted between the fuselage and the engine nacelles, turned through 90°. A series of diving tests were carried out near Friedrichshafen, but after one test, the pilot levelled out at some 2,500 ft. and retracted the dive brakes whereupon the interlinked elevator tabs should have returned to their normal flight position. However, the tabs jammed and the aircraft crashed. In the meantime, Dornier had been delivering the Do 217E-2 to service units with an alternative tail cone packed in the bomb-bay. On arrival at their destination, *Luftwaffe* personnel had simply removed the tail brake and substituted the tail cone. But by the late summer of 1941, the RLM was forced to admit defeat, and all further attempts to utilise the Do 217 in the dive-bombing role were abandoned.

Throughout 1941, deliveries of the Do 217E-2 and E-3 continued to the three *Gruppen* of *Kampfgeschwader* 2 which, by the autumn, were all based along the channel coast for operations against Britain and, in concert with II/KG 40, attacks on Allied shipping in the North Sea. For anti-shipping operations, the 15-mm. MG 151 cannon was replaced by a 20-mm. MG FF cannon, and various minor modifications were introduced by forward maintenance units to improve operational effectiveness. By the end of 1941, approximately 300 Do 217E bombers had been delivered to the *Luftwaffe*. These included the pre-production Do 217E-0s and first few production Do 217E-1s completed in 1940, plus 100 Do 217E-3s, the remainder of the total being made up almost equally of E-1s and E-2s.

Late in 1941, the assembly lines had begun to switch from the Do 217E-2 to the **Do 217E-4** which came into operational use early in 1942. The Do 217E-4 differed from its predecessor in only minor respects, having BMW 801C engines which, unlike the BMW 801MA and ML, were supplied as bare bones power plants rather than as complete power eggs, but possessed similar ratings, and in being fitted with the so-called *Kuto-Nase* balloon-cable cutter in the wing leading edge. A small number of late-production examples of this model were modified on the assembly line as parent aircraft for the Henschel Hs 293A stand-off missile under the designation **Do 217E-5**. They were fitted with an ETC 2000/XII carrier under each outboard wing panel, a Telefunken FuG 203b *Kehl III* transmitter for the missile's FuG 230b *Strassburg* receiver, a *Knüppel* or joystick control box to be manipulated by the bombardier for line-of-sight guidance, and the necessary warm air hoses in the wings to maintain the missile's interior temperature at a constant level. A number of Do 217E-5s were subsequently used by the *Lehr und Erprobungskommando* 36 at Garz, Usedom, on the Baltic coast, this unit having the task of bringing the Hs 293 and FX 1400 missiles up to operational status and training personnel in their use, and others operated by II/KG 100 launched the first Hs 293As operationally against Allied destroyers in the Bay of Biscay on August 25, 1943.

DORNIER DO 217K AND DO 217M

The designations Do 217F and G had been reserved for two 1941 derivatives of the basic design which were not proceeded with, and the **Do 217H** was a conversion of the 21st production Do 217E with DB 601 engines fitted with experimental turbo-superchargers undertaken in September 1941 by Daimler-Benz at the *Erprobungsstelle* Echterdingen for high-altitude trials. The Do 217J was an interim night fighter derivative of the Do 217E-2, and thus

Do 217K-1s (Werk-Nr. 4518 above and 4487 below) of Kampfgeschwader 2 (1943)

the next production bomber version was the **Do 217K-1** which began flight trials in March 1942.

The Do 217K-1 differed markedly from its predecessors, the most noteworthy innovation being an entirely redesigned forward fuselage from which the stepped windscreen was eliminated, the glazed panelling being extended forward to the extreme nose. The BMW 801C engines were supplanted by BMW 801Ds which, operating on 96 octane fuel, each offered 1,700 h.p. for take-off and 1,440 h.p. at 18,700 ft. Defensive armament comprised an MG 81Z (twin 7.9-mm. MG 81 machine guns) with 1,000 rounds in the nose, a 13-mm. MG 131 with 500 rounds in the electrically-operated dorsal turret, a similar weapon with 1,000 rounds in the lower rear position, and two (later four) MG 81s with 750 r.p.g. in lateral positions.

The Do 217K was intended primarily for the night bombing role, and the initial production model, the Do 217K-1 which began to leave the assembly line in the late summer of 1942, entering service with *Kampfgeschwader* 2 in the autumn, was preceded by three prototypes, the first of which, the **Do 217K V1**, was briefly flown with an experimental single fin-and-rudder assembly, and the third, the **Do 217K V3**, was later used as a carrier aircraft for the DFS 228 V1 high-altitude reconnaissance sailplane. The Do 217 K-1 was the first model to adopt as standard the R25 tail fairing housing a Perlon braking chute, and in 1944 experiments were con-

26

A Do 217K-1 bearing the emblem of Luftflotte 2 which indicated that it was subordinated directly to Luftflotte Headquarters. Note lack of tailwheel doors

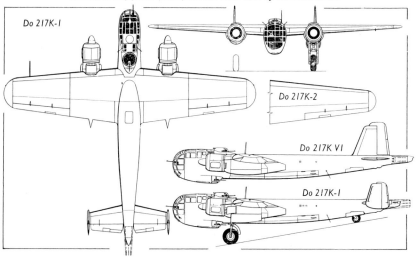

Do 217K-1

Do 217K-2

Do 217K VI

Do 217K-1

A Do 217K-2 (Werk-Nr. 4572), this version having the extended wing and being intended specifically as a carrier for the FX 1400 Fritz X

ducted with a Do 217K-1 fitted with ETC 2000/XII carriers both under the outboard wing panels (R10) and between the fuselage and engine nacelles (R15) to enable the aircraft to carry no fewer than four L5 torpedoes, although it was not used operationally with this warload.

Towards the end of 1942, a version of the bomber intended specifically to carry the FX 1400 *Fritz X* stand-off missile, the **Do 217K-2**, made its début. Equipped with the FuG 203a *Kehl I* transmitter for the missile's FuG 230a *Strassburg* receiver, and ETC 2000/XII carriers between the fuselage and the engine nacelles, the Do 217K-2 introduced extended wing outer panels, increasing overall span from 62 ft. 4 in. to 81 ft. 4½ in. and gross wing area from 613.54 to 721.18 sq. ft. A 255 Imp. gal. auxiliary fuel tank was mounted in the forward bomb-bay (R17) as standard, and the tail cone housed four aft-firing 7.9-mm. MG 81 machine guns (R19). These aft-firing weapons could be supplemented when required by a pair of MG 81s in the tail of each engine nacelle with 250 r.p.m., the entire battery of fixed guns being

fired by the pilot aided by an RF2C periscope with PV1B sighting head.

Do 217K-2s operated by III/KG 100 based on Marseilles-Istres launched their first *Fritz X* missiles in action over the Mediterranean on August 29, 1943, only four days after the operational début of the Hs 293A with II/KG 100. The **Do 217K-3** was essentially similar to the K-2 but was fitted with the later FuG 203c or 203d *Kehl IV* transmitter enabling it to carry either the Hs 293A or *Fritz X* with equal facility.

During the spring of 1943, two prototypes of a modified version of the Do 217K with re-arranged cockpit and defensive armament were tested at Dornier's Löwenthal plant as the **Do 217L V1** and **V2**, but no production of this variant was undertaken, the last bomber model of the basic design to be built in any quantity being the Do 217M manufactured in parallel with the Do 217K. During 1942, in order to safeguard against production delays resulting from shortages of BMW 801D engines, Dornier adapted the Do 217K-1 airframe to take Daimler-Benz DB 603A engines as the

Do 217M-1, the two models being manufactured in parallel and entering service virtually simultaneously. The DB 603A was rated at 1,750 h.p. for take-off and 1,620 h.p. at 18,700 ft., and provided the Do 217M-1 with a generally similar performance to that of the BMW 801D-powered model, offensive loads and defensive armament also being similar. An example of the Do 217M-1 (*Werk-Nr* 56051) fell into Allied hands on the night of February 23-24, 1944 when an aircraft of 2./ KG 2 attacking London received minor damage from anti-aircraft fire over the northwest suburbs, the crew promptly baling out at 10,000 ft., and the abandoned aircraft flying on to make an excellent belly landing in Cambridge.

Consideration was given to mounting turbo-superchargers on the Do 217M, and two prototypes, the **Do 217 V13** and **V14**, were actually tested with these but they were not adopted for production models. The **Do 217M-5** was another sub-type that failed to attain series production, this being an Hs 293 carrier with a single missile mounted semi-externally beneath the fuselage, and the **Do 217M-11** embodying similar extended outer wing panels to those of the Do 217K-2 was intended as a long-range missile carrier with either an FX 1400 *Fritz X* or Hs 293A missile mounted

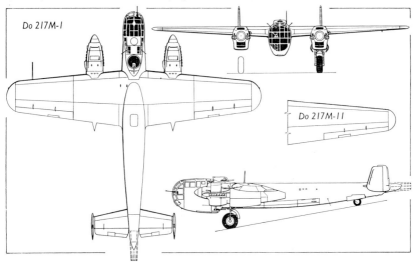

Do 217M-1

Do 217M-11

29

DORNIER DO 217M-1 SPECIFICATION

Type: *Four-seat Heavy Night Bomber.* **Power Plants:** *Two Daimler-Benz DB 603A 12-cylinder liquid-cooled engines each rated at 1,750 h.p. for take-off and 1,850 h.p. at 6,900 ft.* **Armament:** *Two 7.9-mm. MG 81 machine guns with 500 r.p.g. in nose, one 13-mm. MG 131 machine gun with 500 rounds in electrically-operated dorsal turret, one 13-mm. MG 131 machine gun with 1,000 rounds in ventral step, and two 7.9-mm. MG 81 machine guns with 750 r.p.g. in lateral positions. (Offensive) Maximum bomb load of 8,818 lb. (5,550 lb. internally).* **Performance:** *Maximum speed, 294 m.p.h. at sea level, 348 m.p.h. at 18,700 ft.; economical cruising speed, 248 m.p.h.; maximum range on internal fuel, 1,335 mls., with auxiliary fuel, 1,550 mls.; initial climb rate (at normal loaded weight), 690 ft./min.; time to 3,280 ft., 3.3 min., to 6,560 ft., 6.7 min.; service ceiling (with maximum internal bomb load), 24,170 ft., (without bomb load), 31,200 ft.* **Weights:** *Empty, 19,985 lb; empty; equipped, 24,140 lb.; maximum overload, 36,817 lb.* **Dimensions:** *Span, 62 ft. 4 in.; length, 55 ft. 9¼ in., (Do 217M-1/R25), 58 ft. 8 in.; height, 16 ft. 3⅜ in.; wing area, 613 542 sq. ft.*

semi-externally beneath the fuselage. However, by mid-1943 the *Luftwaffe* had a pressing need for additional night fighters and, in consequence, the majority of the Do 217M air-

A Do 217M-1 (Werk-Nr. 56158), formerly operated by KG 2, which was evaluated in the United Kingdom after the surrender

The Do 217M-1 (right) differed from the Do 217K-1 solely in the type of power plants installed, but relatively few M-series aircraft attained service with the Luftwaffe, most airframes being adapted as Do 217N fighters

frames completed were adapted to take a heavy forward-firing cannon armament and were delivered to the *Nachtjagdgruppen* as Do 217N night fighters, relatively few Do 217M-1s thus reaching the *Kampfgruppen*.

With the conversion of the last Do 217M-1 airframe for the night fighting role late in 1943, series production of the Do 217 finally terminated, a grand total of 1,366 bombers and missile carriers and 364 night fighters and intruders having been delivered.

DORNIER DO 217P

Prior to the Do 217 production phase-out late in 1943, Dornier had adapted the basic airframe for operation at extreme altitudes as both a bomber and reconnaissance aircraft under the designation Do 217P. Retaining the wing, tail assembly, basic fuselage structure and undercarriage of the Do 217E-2, the first prototype of the high-altitude model, the **Do 217P V1** was powered by two Daimler-Benz DB 603B engines supercharged by a DB 605T engine, this arrangement being known as an *HZ-*

Anlage and offering a total of 3,500 h.p. for take-off, 3,720 h.p. at 6,900 ft., and 3,240 h.p. at 18,700 ft. For climb and combat a total of 2,880 h.p. was available at 45,000 ft., and maximum cruising power at the same altitude was 2,640 h.p. The DB 605T, which drove a two-stage supercharger, was installed in the centre fuselage. Large intercooler radiators were slung beneath the wing, between the fuselage and the engine nacelles, and air scoops for the blower and DB 605T engine were located below the fuselage, just aft of the wing trailing edge. The four crew members were housed ahead of the wing in a pressure cabin built in the form of a detachable compartment, this being extensively glazed by flat panels, and a Perlon tail braking chute was fitted.

The Do 217P V1 was flown for the first time in June 1942, and during the course of flight trials attained an altitude of 43,960 ft. Two additional prototypes, the **Do 217P V2** and **V3**, joined the test programme during the summer and autumn of 1942, these differing from the V1 primarily in having extended outer wing panels which increased overall span to 80 ft. 4½ in. and gross wing area to 720 sq. ft. By the beginning of 1943, three pre-production **Do 217P-0** reconnaissance-bombers were under construction, the first of these being flown during the early summer and the remaining two being completed during the autumn, all three being flown to the *Erprobungsstelle* Rechlin late in 1943 for official evaluation.

The Do 217P-0 was primarily a reconnaissance aircraft intended to operate at altitudes at which it would be immune from interception, and its defensive armament, which comprised a pair of forward-firing MG 81 machine guns and a similar pair of weapons firing aft above and below the fuselage, only intended for use at lower altitudes owing to the problem of sealing the gun openings. A single Rb 20/30 camera was installed in the fuselage immediately aft of the pressurized compartment, and two automatic Rb 75/30 cameras were mounted in the aft end of the centre fuselage. For the bombing role it was proposed that two 1,102-lb. bombs should be slung from racks under the outboard

(Above, below and at top of opposite page) The Do 217P V1 (BK-IR) which, featuring the HZ-Anlage, was first flown in June 1942

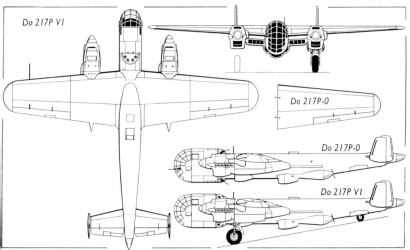

Do 217P VI

Do 217P-0

Do 217P-0

Do 217P VI

33

DORNIER DO 217P-0
SPECIFICATION

Type: *Three-seat High-Altitude Reconnaissance-Bomber.* **Power Plants:** *Two Daimler-Benz DB 603B twelve-cylinder liquid-cooled engines (supercharged by a Daimler-Benz DB 605T) each rated at 1,750 h.p. for take-off, 1,860 h.p. at 6,900 ft., and 1,440 h.p. at 45,000 ft.* **Armament:** *Two forward-firing 7.9-mm. MG 81 machine guns, two 7.9-mm. MG 81 machine guns in each of two aft-firing positions above and below fuselage. (Offensive) Two 1,102-lb. bombs on underwing racks.* **Performance:** *Maximum speed (at 29,250 lb.), 488 m.p.h. at 46,000 ft.; initial climb rate (at 31,600 lb.), 955 ft./min.; time to 29,400 ft., 19.6 min.; service ceiling (at 29,250 lb.), 53,000 ft., (at 30,700 lb.), 50,800 ft.* **Weights:** *Normal loaded, 31,600 lb.; maximum overload, 35,200 lb.* **Dimensions:** *Span, 80 ft. 4½ in.; length, 58 ft. 10½ in.; wing area, 720 sq. ft.*

wing panels, and for long-range reconnaissance sorties these racks were to be occupied by 198 Imp. gal. auxiliary tanks.

The trio of Do 217P-0 aircraft was exhaustively tested at Rechlin, but plans for quantity production failed to materialize.

DORNIER DO 217R

In the summer of 1944, III/KG 100 based at Orleans/Bricy was the recipient of five aircraft designated **Do 217R**. Intended to launch Hs 293A missiles, the five Do 217Rs were, in fact, five of the six Do 317A prototypes which had been completed without cabin pressurization equipment after initial trials with the Do 317 V1 had yielded somewhat disappointing results in the high altitude role. As Do 217R missile-carriers, these aircraft carried a defensive armament of a single 13-mm. MG 131 machine gun in an electrically-operated turret in the cabin roof, a fixed forward-firing 15-mm. MG 151 cannon in the lower port side of the forward fuselage, a pair of free-mounted 7.9-mm. MG 81 machine guns projecting from the starboard side of the nose glazing, and two aft-firing 13-mm. MG 131 machine guns on free mountings above and below the fuselage. The offensive load comprised a pair of Hs 293A missiles, one outboard of each engine nacelle.

There is no record of any operational use of the Do 217R, and as III/KG 100 was disbanded in August 1944 for retraining on fighters, if the Do 217R *did* see active service, it is improbable that more than a few sorties were flown.

OPERATIONAL CAREER

Only one complete *Kampfgeschwader* was destined to be equipped with the Do 217, this being KG 2 of which II *Gruppe* had remained in the West when the assault on the Soviet Union began on June 22, 1941 in order to complete conversion from the Do 17Z to the Do 217E. *Kampfgeschwader* 2's III *Gruppe* actually began conversion from the Do 17Z to the Do 217E while still in Russia, but this was pulled back during the autumn of 1941 to complete re-equipment, and was followed by KG 2's remaining component, II *Gruppe*, and during the remaining months of 1941 the entire *Kampfgeschwader* converted and was based in the Netherlands, at Gilze Rijen and Eindhoven, by early 1942 for bombing raids over England and anti-shipping strikes in the North Sea. KG 2 was destined to remain in the Netherlands with its Do 217s until September 1944, participating in the retaliatory "Little Blitz" in that year under the direction of the *Angriffsführer England*.

Kampfgeschwader 40 had, in fact, preceded

(*Right*) *A Do 217K-1 (Werk-Nr. 4429) attached to Luftflotte 2 Headquarters*

KG 2 into action with the Do 217E, II/KG 40 commencing operations against North Sea shipping under the tactical command of the *Fliegerführer Atlantik* in the spring of 1941 from Soesterberg in the Netherlands, the remaining two *Gruppen* operating the Fw 200C Condor. Early in 1943, II/KG 40 gave up its Do 217s and was redesignated V/KG 2 with Me 410s, IV/KG 2 being formed about the same time on Do 217s to give *Kampfgeschwader* four Do 217-equipped *Gruppen* and one Me 410-equipped *Gruppe*, a new II/KG 40 being formed on He 177As. The KG 2 *Gruppen* were equipped with a succession of Do 217 variants, including the E-1, E-2, E-3, K-1 and M-1, undertaking sporadic day and night attacks on Britain but concentrating their efforts primarily against Allied shipping.

In April 1943, II/KG 100 re-equipped with Hs 293-carrying Do 217E-5s while III/KG 100, formed from the *Lehr- und Erpobungskommando* 1, equipped with the *Fritz X*-carrying Do 217K-2, these *Gruppen* commencing operations in the Bay of Biscay on August 25, 1943 and the Mediterranean on August 29, 1943 respectively. The Do 217K-2s succeeded in hitting the battleships *Roma* and *Italia* on September 9, 1943 with *Fritz X* missiles, and the III/KG 100 aircraft were active in opposing the Salerno landings throughout the following week, scoring hits on the cruiser U.S.S. *Savannah* and several supply vessels, and subsequently damaging the battleship H.M.S. *Warspite* with *Fritz X* missiles. In January 1944, III/KG 100's Do 217K-2s sank the cruiser H.M.S. *Spartan* and the destroyer H.M.S. *Janus*.

Other units operating the Do 217 included one of the *Staffeln* of I/KG 66 which undertook operations over the British Isles between January 1943 and January 1945, and III/KG 66 which was formed late in 1944 from a Do 217 training unit, 5./KG 101. It fell to the *Versuchskommando* of KG 200 to undertake the last missile attack with Do 217s, 12 aircraft from this unit launching their Hs 293s against the Oder bridges on April 12, 1945.

DORNIER DO 317

When the *Führungsstab der Luftwaffe* drafted its so-called "Bomber B" requirement which was translated into a specification for issue to selected airframe manufacturers in July 1939 by the *Technische Amt* of the *Reichs-luftfahrtministerium* (RLM), its intention was not merely the provision of successors for the Junkers Ju 88 and Heinkel He 111; its aim was also to carry the state of the art in medium bomber design a significant step forward.

The specification was noteworthy in the performance advances that it stipulated, and equally so in the design innovations that it called for. The "Bomber B" had to possess a range of 2,237 miles to endow it with a radius of action sufficient to encompass the entire British Isles from bases that it was assumed would be available in France and Norway, a maximum speed of 373 m.p.h at 19,685-22,965 ft

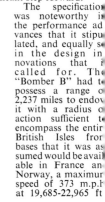

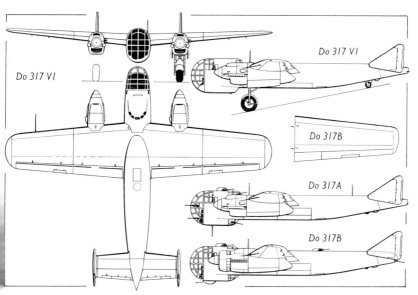

Do 317 V1

Do 317 V1

Do 317B

Do 317A

Do 317B

which compared favourably with the speeds of the best contemporary fighters, and a bomb load of 4,410 lb. It had to carry three or four crew members, possess a loaded weight of the order of 44,090 lb., and be of twin-engine configuration, utilizing the extremely advanced 24-cylinder liquid-cooled Daimler-Benz DB 604 or Junkers Jumo 222 engines then at an early stage in development, but the really radical demands of the specification were its insistence on pressurized accommodation for the crew, and the use of remotely-controlled barbettes to house defensive armament.

Initially, the specification was issued to four manufacturers; Arado, Dornier, Focke-Wulf and Junkers, although the scope of the contest was later to be broadened to include Henschel when it was realized by the RLM that this company had more pressure cabin experience than any of the other contestants, with the possible exception of Junkers. The final proposals of the original four competing companies were submitted to the *Technische Amt* in July 1940, and evaluation eliminated

The Do 317 V1 (VK-IY) was the sole prototype completed as a high-altitude bomber, the remaining five examples being completed without cabin pressurization equipment as Do 217R bombers

the Arado contender, the Ar 340, prototypes being ordered of each of the other submissions, the Do 317, the Fw 191 and the Ju 288.

Dornier's proposal was based broadly on the design of the Do 217 then undergoing prototype trials, the four crew members being housed ahead of the wing in a pressure cabin which, taking the form of a detachable compartment pressurized by tapping the superchargers of the DB 604 engines, was extensively glazed by a series of flat panels. The *Technische Amt* considered the technically more advanced projects tendered by Focke-Wulf and Junkers more promising than the Do 317, and Dornier was instructed to embody some of the features proposed for its "Bomber B" in a new high-altitude version of the Do 217. Some design development of the Do 317 continued without priority as a possible back-up for the Fw 191 and Ju 288, but after attaining the mock-up

stage in 1940, further work was stopped to permit concentration on the Do 217P high-altitude reconnaissance bomber.

In 1941, the Do 317 was resurrected and offered to the RLM as a potential production successor to the Do 217. Two versions were proposed: the simplified and less ambitious **Do 317A** powered by two DB 603A engines and featuring conventional defensive armament, and the more advanced **Do 317B** with DB 610 engines, remotely-controlled defensive barbettes, and an extended wing. Six prototypes of the Do 317A were ordered, and the first of these, the **Do 317 V1** (VK-IY), commenced its flight test programme in 1943. Following closely the structural design of the Do 217, the Do 317 V1 featured an all-metal two-spar wing carrying slotted ailerons interlinked with electrically-operated split flaps, and accommodating a 343 Imp. gal. fuel tank between the spars on each side of the fuselage, inboard of the engine nacelles, and a 47 Imp. gal. tank immediately outboard of each nacelle. The oval-section fuselage housed a further 462 Imp. gal. of fuel in a main tank immediately aft of the pressure cabin and above the bomb-bay which was designed to accept a maximum load of six 1,102-lb. bombs. The DB 603A 12-cylinder liquid-cooled engines were each rated at 1,750 h.p. for take-off, and although no provision for defensive armament was made in the Do 317 V1, the production Do 317A was to have featured a single 13-mm. MG 131 machine gun in an electrically-operated turret in the roof of the pressure cabin, a fixed forward-firing 15-mm. MG 151 cannon in the lower port side of the forward fuselage, a pair of free-mounted 7.9-mm. MG 81 machine guns projecting from the starboard side of the nose glazing, and two aft-firing 13-mm. MG 131 machine guns on free mountings, one above and the other below the fuselage.

Trials with the Do 317 V1 revealed no real performance advance over the Do 217P-0, and the decision was taken, therefore, to complete the remaining five prototypes without cabin pressurization equipment and employ them as Hs 293A missile carriers. In this form the prototypes were redesignated Do 217R, and subsequently saw service with III/KG 100 at Orleans/Bricy. At this time, the Do 317B project had attained the full-scale mock-up stage, but the *Technische Amt* concluded that it lacked sufficient promise to warrant further development, and thus the entire Do 317 programme was cancelled. The Do 317B was intended to utilize the same basic airframe as the Do 317A, but wing span was increased by 17 ft. 7 in. by the introduction of new outer panels, wing fuel tankage was increased, maximum bomb load was raised to 12,346 lb., and defensive armament was intended to consist of a chin barbette housing twin 7.9-mm. MG 81 machine guns, a dorsal barbette containing two 13-mm. MG 131 machine guns a manned forward turret containing a similar pair of weapons, and a remotely-controlled 20-mm. MG 151 cannon in the extreme tail.

DORNIER DO 317B SPECIFICATION

(This specification is based on manufacturer's estimates, and data in parentheses applies specifically to the Do 317A)

Type: *Four-seat High-Altitude Heavy Bomber.* **Power Plants:** *Two Daimler-Benz DB 610A/B (DB 603) 24 (12)-cylinder liquid-cooled engines each rated at 2,870 (1,750) h.p. for take-off and 2,560 (1,625) h.p. at 25,000 (18,700) ft.* **Armament:** *One electrically-operated upper turret with two 13-mm. MG 131 machine guns, one remotely-controlled chin barbette containing two 7.9-mm. MG 81 machine guns, one remotely-controlled dorsal barbette containing two 13-mm. MG 131 machine guns, and one remotely-controlled 20-mm. MG 151 cannon in extreme tail. (Offensive) Maximum internal bomb load of 12,346 lb. plus two 3,968-lb. bombs on underwing racks. Typical loads (internal) included four 3,086-lb. or two 3,968-lb. bombs, or two 3,086-lb. bombs and a 352 Imp. gal. auxiliary fuel tank in forward bomb-bay.* **Performance:** *Maximum speed, 416 m.p.h. at 25,000 ft.; maximum cruising speed, 335 m.p.h.; maximum range on standard internal fuel, 2,237 mls., with auxiliary tank in forward bomb-bay, 2,485 mls.; service ceiling, 34,500 ft.* **Weights:** *Maximum loaded, 52,910 lb.* **Dimensions:** *Span, 85 (67) ft. 3½ (8½) in.; length, 55 ft. 1½ in.; height, 17 ft. 10½ in.*

On December 28, 1936, the keel of "Carrier A" was laid on Slip Number One at the Deutsche Werke Kiel, and within a few weeks the *Technische Amt* of the *Reichsluftfahrtministerium* (RLM) had evolved a specification for a two-seat multi-purpose aircraft intended to operate from the new vessel. Issued to selected manufacturers, the specification called for an all-metal biplane with folding wings and stressed for diving attacks at speeds up to 373 m.p.h. It had to be capable of carrying a single torpedo or a minimum bomb load of 1,100 lb. at maximum and cruising speeds of at least 186 and 155 m.p.h. respectively, and it had to have a range of 620 miles; defensive armament was to comprise a fixed forward-firing 7.9-mm. MG 17 machine gun with an MG 15 of similar calibre on a flexible mounting for the second crew member; design accent was to be placed on maximum crew visibility; the undercarriage had to be jettisonable for emergency ditching,

and provision had to be made for flotation equipment.

Both the Arado and Fieseler companies submitted proposals aimed at meeting the requirements of the specification, and three prototypes were ordered from each company, the projects being designated Ar 195 and Fi 167 respectively. Prototypes of both aircraft were completed during the summer of 1938, but the Ar 195 was soon found to be incapable of meeting the performance demands of the specification. The Fi 167, on the other hand, was found to be able to improve on the specification in every respect and, in consequence, a pre-production series of 12 examples of the Fieseler design was promptly ordered.

Designed by Reinhold Mewes who had placed emphasis on ease of manufacture and maintenance, the **Fi 167** was a somewhat angular two-bay biplane. The entire engine installation could be exposed for servicing by

(Left) The Fi 167 V1 began flight trials in the summer of 1938 in competition with the Ar 195 V1

The Fi 167A-0, the fifth pre-production example of this shipboard torpedo-bomber and reconnaissance aircraft

the removal of a series of light metal panels; the centre fuselage was covered by light alloy sheet, and the aft fuselage was a stressed-skin monocoque. The two-spar mainplanes were braced by two pairs of inclined N-struts, a pair of splayed N-struts supporting the upper mainplane centre section above the fuselage, and the wings were hinged to fold aft immediately outboard of the inner pair of interplane struts. Full-span leading-edge automatic slats were fitted to both upper and lower mainplanes, the latter also carrying large-area trailing-edge flaps, and the robust undercarriage featured long-stroke shock absorber legs to cater for high descent rates.

Flight trials revealed the fact that the **Fi 167** V1 possessed truly exceptional low-speed characteristics, and throttled back and with elevators fully up, the aircraft simply sank slowly and almost vertically. On one occasion, with Gerhard Fieseler at the controls, the aircraft "sank" 9,800 ft. to an altitude of a 100 ft. above the ground while remaining continuously over one spot. At the other end of the performance scale, the Fi 167 V1 improved on the stipulated maximum speed, and proved capable of carrying double the offensive load called for by the specification. Indeed, so successful were initial trials that Fieseler decided that it was unnecessary to complete the third prototype, and immediately initiated preparation for the construction of the 12

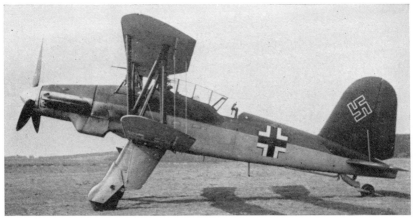

(*Above and below left*) *Pre-production Fi 167A-0s which underwent operational suitability trials with the Erprobungsstaffel 167 during the summer of* 1940

pre-production Fi 167A-0 aircraft.

The pre-production aircraft differed little from the Fi 167 V1 and V2, the primary changes resulting from tests at the *Erprobungsstelle* at Rechlin being the introduction of larger low-pressure tyres, new flame-damper exhaust outlets and modified supercharger air intake for the DB 601B engine, and the provision of Flettner tabs on the rudder and elevators. Other changes included an improved emergency release mechanism for the main undercarriage members, spring-loaded bolts being released electrically, and the provision of an inflatable two-man dinghy in the wing.

In the meantime, "Carrier A" had been christened *Graf Zeppelin* and launched on December 8, 1938, but as it was not anticipated that this vessel would be commissioned before the summer of 1940, construction of the **Fi 167A-0** received no special priority, and the Fi 167A-01 (TJ-AJ) did not commence its flight test programme until the early months of that year. By this time, the *Technische Amt* had decided that the shipboard dive bomber role would be performed by the Junkers Ju 87C-0, thus restricting the Fi 167A to the tasks of torpedo-bombing and reconnaissance, and a further blow was dealt the Fieseler biplane's prospects when, in May 1940, construction of the *Graf Zeppelin* was halted. Nevertheless,

the manufacture of the 12 Fi 167A-0 aircraft was continued, and all aircraft of the batch were accepted by the *Luftwaffe* during the summer of 1940, the *Erprobungsstaffel* 167 being formed for operational suitability trials. Late in September 1941, the 11th Fi 167A-0 (KC-QE) was loaned to the Daimler-Benz *Erprobungsstelle* at Echterdingen for various engine trials, and by May 13, 1942, when the order was given to resume construction of the *Graf Zeppelin*, the *Erprobungsstaffel* 167 with nine Fi 167s on strength had been transferred

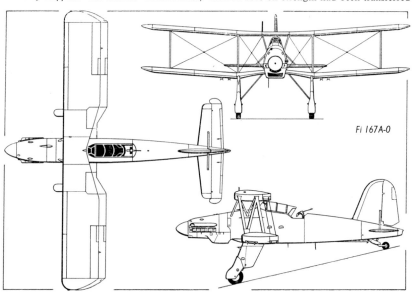

Fi 167A-0

as potential equipment for Germany's first carrier, for by the time the *Luftwaffe* resumed the training of shipboard squadrons, a decision had been taken to adapt the Ju 87D as a torpedo-bomber under the designation Ju 87E.

The Fi 167s remained in the Netherlands until early in 1943, participating in several experimental programmes, including one intended to evolve the most effective camouflage pattern for aircraft operating over the sea, the *Erprobungsstaffel 167* then returning to Germany where it was disbanded. The Fi 167s were returned to Fieseler for overhaul, three subsequently being delivered to the *Fahrwerkserprobungsstelle der DVL*, the DVL's undercarriage test centre at Budweis, where they were used for measuring landing shocks under various load conditions, flying both in standard biplane configuration and as highly-loaded sesquiplanes, the lower mainplanes being detached immediately outboard of the undercarriage, additional struts supporting the upper mainplanes. The few remaining Fi 167s were sold to the Rumanian government, their fate after their arrival in Rumania being unknown.

to the Netherlands for what were referred to as "advanced service trials" in Dutch coastal areas. However, the Fieseler biplane, despite its unique qualities, was no longer considered

---

FIESELER FI 167A-O SPECIFICATION

Type: *Two-seat Shipboard Torpedo-Bomber and Reconnaissance Aircraft.* **Power Plant:** *One Daimler-Benz DB 601 B 12-cylinder liquid-cooled engine rated at 1,100 h.p. for take-off and 1,020 h.p. at 14,765 ft.* **Armament:** *(Defensive) One fixed forward-firing 7.9-mm. MG 17 machine gun with 500 rounds in starboard side of forward fuselage and one 7.9-mm. MG 15 machine gun on flexible mounting in observer's cockpit with 600 rounds. (Offensive) Normal load comprising four 110-lb. SC 50 bombs plus one 551-lb. SC 250 or 1,102-lb. bomb, or maximum load comprising one 2,205-lb. SD 1000 bomb or one 1,686.5-lb. LT F5b torpedo.* **Performance:** *Maximum speed (as bomber), 199 m.p.h., (as reconnaissance aircraft), 202 m.p.h.; normal crusing speed, 155 m.p.h.; maximum cruising speed, 168 m.p.h.; range, 808 mls., (as reconnaissance aircraft with 66 Imp. gal. drop tank), 932 mls.; service ceiling, 24,600-26,900 ft.* **Weights:** *Empty, 6,173 lb.; normal loaded, 9,920 lb.; maximum, 10,690 lb.* **Dimensions:** *Span, 44 ft. 3½ in.; length, 37 ft. 4¾ in. height, 15 ft. 9 in.; wing area, 489.76 sq. ft.*

FOCKE-WULF FW 189

When, in 1941, the press department of the *Reichsluftfahrtministerium* (RLM) revealed publicly the existence of the Focke-Wulf Fw 189A tactical reconnaissance and army co-operation monoplane, it bestowed the appropriate enough sobriquet of *"Das Fliegende Auge"* on this newcomer to the ranks of the *Aufklärungsstaffeln* (H), for, on the Eastern Front at least, the Fw 189A was destined to become literally "The Flying Eye" of the *Wehrmacht*. It was to prove supremely versatile, universally popular with its pilots, and one of the most reliable aircraft ever to see *Luftwaffe* service, yet it was conceived at a time when few thought in terms of anything other than the classic single-engined high-wing monoplane formula as the best solution to the demands of the tasks for which the Fw 189 was conceived.

In February 1937, the first prototype of the Henschel Hs 126 was undergoing initial trials and bid fair to provide the *Luftwaffe* with the required replacement for the Heinkel He 46 in the *Aufklärungsstaffeln* (H), but the *Technische Amt* of the RLM was already looking further ahead and, in that month, issued a completely new specification which demanded an appreciably more advanced aircraft than the Henschel; a tactical reconnaissance aircraft carrying three crew members, offering all-round defensive cover and possessing a rather higher performance than anything previously envisaged for aircraft in this category.

The specification was issued to three manufacturers—Arado, the Hamburger Flugzeugbau and Focke-Wulf—and no specification could have resulted in three more dissimilar proposals to meet a single requirement. The Arado team proved the least venturesome, electing to retain the classic high-wing formula in the belief that no other acceptable arrangement could offer a comparable all-round view. The Hamburger Flugzeugbau proposed so revolutionary a solution, the single-engined

The Fw 189 V1 photographed shortly before initial flight trials in July 1938. This aircraft was subsequently registered D-OPVN

(Left) The Fw 189 V1 (D-OPVN) prior to withdrawal from the test programme late in 1938 for conversion as the Fw 189 V1b

asymmetrical Ha 141, that, initially, the *Technische Amt* refused to take the proposal seriously, regarding it as a degenerate expression of the designer's art, and Focke-Wulf tendered a proposal for a *twin*-engined aircraft with twin tailbooms and an extensively-glazed central fuselage nacelle.

From the drawing-board of Dipl.Ing. Kurt Tank, the Focke-Wulf project took the *Technische Amt* somewhat by surprise as this organisation had visualized a single-engined solution to its tactical reconnaissance requirement, although, in fact, the specification had merely suggested the desirable power and not stipulated that this should be derived from one engine. The merits of the Focke-Wulf proposal were soon apparent to the less bigoted personnel of the *Technische Amt*, as were also the advantages inherent in a highly unorthodox suggestion appended by Tank to the submission—that interchangeable fuselage nacelles be developed so that, while retaining the same power plant, wings, undercarriage, tailbooms and tail assembly, the same basic aircraft could fulfil a variety of roles ranging from close support to crew training.

The *Technische Amt*, like most such organisations, possessed its share of conventionalists as well as its visionaries, and the former viewed the twin-boom arrangement of the Focke-Wulf proposal with suspicion, protesting that this configuration must perforce be heavier than an orthodox fuselage, and that the open frame formed by the tailbooms would be subject to distortion under the stresses of violent manoeuvres. Therefore, late in April 1937, contracts were awarded to both Arado and Focke-Wulf for the construction of three prototypes of their respective projects, these

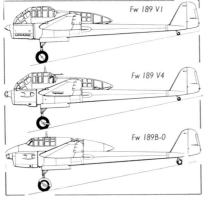

Fw 189 V1

Fw 189 V4

Fw 189B-0

being allocated the official RLM type numbers Ar 198 and Fw 189.

Prototype construction in the charge of Dipl.Ing. E. Kosel began immediately, and the **Fw 189 V1** (D-OPVN) flew for the first time 15 months later, in July 1938, with the designer, Kurt Tank, at the controls. The Fw 189 V1 was powered by two pre-production Argus As 410 12-cylinder inverted-vee air-cooled engines each rated at 430 h.p. for take-off and driving two-bladed fixed-pitch air-screws, and this was joined by the second proto-type, the **Fw 189 V2** (D-OVHD), in August and the third, the **Fw 189 V3** (D-ORMH), in September 1938. From the outset of the flight test programme the prototypes met the most sanguine expectations of the design team, and Tank promptly christened the aircraft *Eule* (Owl), although this was destined to be supplanted by the popular onomatopœic appellation of "*Uhu*" in service.

A low-wing cantilever monoplane, the Fw

(Right and below) The third prototype, the Fw 189 V3, which joined the flight test pro-gramme in September 1938

47

189 was of all-metal construction. The three-spar stressed-skin wings comprised a rectangular centre section between the tailbooms supporting the crew nacelle on the centreline, the main and rear spars passing through the nacelle, and tapered outer panels attached to the centre section by bolts along the wing contour between the main and front spars as well as at the main spar. Electrically-operated fabric-covered split trailing-edge flaps were carried between the ailerons and the tailbooms and across the entire centre section. The interchangeable oval-section tailbooms carried the engine nacelles, housed the two 48.4 Imp.gal. fuel tanks and terminated in stressed-skin vertical fins which supported the tailplane between them. The rudders and elevators were metal-framed and fabric-covered. The hydraulically-actuated main undercarriage members were raised aft into the engine nacelles and enclosed by hinged doors, and the tailwheel retracted laterally into the underside of the tailplane.

The Fw 189 V2 was essentially similar to the V1 but was equipped for armament trials, one 7.9-mm. MG 15 machine gun being mounted in the glazed nose and similar

weapons firing from the dorsal step and the nacelle tail cone, two 7.9-mm. MG 17s were mounted in the wing roots, and four ETC racks for a total of four 110-lb. bombs were mounted beneath the outer wing panels. The Fw 189 V3 was not fitted with armament but was the first prototype to receive the automatic variable-pitch Argus airscrew and the so-called *Einheitstriebwerk* (Standard Unit) As 410 engine.

The successful outcome of initial trials with this trio of prototypes and the generally satisfactory results achieved with the Arado Ar 198 had resulted in an order for four additional prototypes of the Fw 189. The first of these, the **Fw 189 V4** (D-OCHO), was intended as a production prototype for the planned A-series of short-range reconnaissance aircraft, and, completed late in 1938, embodied minor changes such as revised engine cowlings, modified defensive armament (which was restricted to a pair of MG 15 machine guns on flexible mountings), semi-cowled mainwheels and an enlarged tailwheel. After completing factory trials, the Fw 189 V4 served as a test vehicle for various types of "special equipment", including the Type

(Above and below) An Fw 189B-0 (Werk-Nr. 0010) trainer. Three pre-production Fw 189B-0s and 10 production Fw 189B-1s were built

S 125 smoke-screen apparatus, and spray containers for chemical warfare substances such as "Lost" (the cover name for one of the "Yellow Cross" group of chemicals, i.e., mustard gas compounds) which could be hung beneath the outer panels in place of the ETC bomb racks.

FOCKE-WULF FW 189B

The second aircraft in the additional batch of four prototypes, the **Fw 189 V5**, was intended as the prototype for the planned B-series of trainers, and featured an entirely redesigned fuselage nacelle of refined aerodynamic shape with an orthodox stepped windscreen. Dual

controls were fitted and all armament was deleted, and the prototype was flown early in 1939. The order to commence series production of the Fw 189A reconnaissance aircraft in the summer of 1939 did not materialise as the *Oberkommando der Luftwaffe* was perfectly satisfied with the Henschel Hs 126 with which it was still in process of re-equipping the *Aufklärungsstaffeln (H)*, but Focke-Wulf did receive instructions to proceed with a pre-production batch of three **Fw 189B-0** trainers and 10 production **Fw 189B-1s**, delivering the pre-production machines and three of the Fw 189B-1s before the end of 1939. The remaining seven of these dual-control five-seaters were completed during January and February 1940, and subsequently delivered to the *Luftwaffe*.

Both landplane and twin-float seaplane variants of the trainer had originally been proposed, the float version being designated **Fw 189D**, the last of the additional batch of four prototypes, the **Fw 187 V7**, being ordered as a seaplane. The Fw 187 V7 was under construction late in 1938, employing an essentially similar airframe to that of the V5, but as a result of changes in seaplane procurement policy this aircraft was cancelled, the partly-built airframe being completed as an Fw 189B-0.

FOCKE-WULF FW 189C

The Fw 189 V1 was withdrawn from the flight test programme late in 1938 and returned to the Focke-Wulf experimental shop for conversion for the assault or close-support role. The original fuselage nacelle was removed and replaced by an armoured nacelle just sufficient in size to accommodate the pilot and a rear gunner seated back to back. The pilot peered through tiny armour-glass panels in an aft-hinged armoured hood, and the gunner was supposed to wield a single 7.9-mm. MG 15 machine gun through a small opening in an armoured visor.

With these changes and designated **Fw 189 V1b**, the prototype resumed flight trials in the spring of 1939, but results were sorely disappointing. The heavily-armoured central nacelle markedly changed the handling characteristics for the worse, performance was sluggish, and the test pilot reported that forward vision was totally inadequate, while the flight observer declared that from the aft seat a gunner would have difficulty in seeing an enemy fighter sitting on his tail. The Fw 189 V1b was therefore returned to the experimental shop for modifications, the armour-glass panels in the pilot's hood being enlarged, and the gunner's visor being replaced by an armoured embrasure offering improved aft vision and limited lateral vision.

Following these further modifications, the Fw 189 V1b undertook comparative trials with the Henschel Hs 129 V2 and V3 which had been built to meet the same assault aircraft requirement, but the results were inconclusive. While the Hs 129 was favoured on the score of size, the overall dimensions of this single-seater presenting a smaller target to ground defences, it offered its pilot an even poorer view than that enjoyed by the pilot of the competing Focke-Wulf aircraft, and while the flying characteristics of the Fw 189 V1b were poor, those of the Hs 129 were execrable. Shortly afterwards, the Fw 189 V1b was written off when, during a demonstration at Bremen, the pilot avoided collision with a hangar which he had not seen until the last moment by pancaking the aircraft heavily.

However, the third of the additional four prototypes, the **Fw 189 V6**, had been ordered as a prototype for the **Fw 189C** assault model, and this was completed at the beginning of 1940. The armoured central nacelle was essentially similar to the definitive nacelle tested on the Fw 189 V1b, Argus As 410A-1 engines offering 465 h.p. for take-off

(Above, right and at foot of page) The Fw 189 V1b in its original form with small glazed panels for the pilot and armoured visor for the gunner

and driving variable-pitch airscrews supplanted the pre-production As 410s with their fixed-pitch airscrews, a new undercarriage was introduced with twin oleo legs for the main members, and a new wing centre section was fitted. This centre section housed two 20-mm. MG FF cannon and four 7.9-mm. MG 17 machine guns, and the rear gunner was provided with a pair of 7.9-mm. MG 81 machine guns on a flexible mounting.

In the meantime, Henschel had begun construction of a pre-production batch of Hs 129A-0 assault aircraft, and by September 1940, when the Fw 189 V6 reached the *Erprobungsstelle* Rechlin, service suitability trials with these were already being undertaken

(*Above and left*) *The Fw 189 V1b with revised armoured nacelle intended to provide better vision for both pilot and rear gunner*

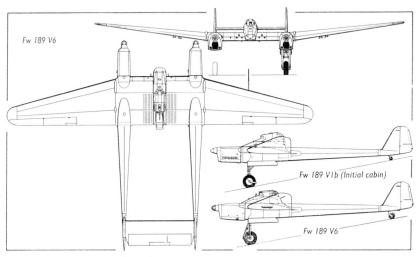

Fw 189 V6

Fw 189 V1b (Initial cabin)

Fw 189 V6

by 5.(*Schlacht*) *Staffel* of *Lehrgeschwader* 2, and while the service pilots were proving vociferous in their condemnation of the Henschel, the RLM concluded that various improvements proposed for the aircraft coupled with the fact that its unit cost was barely more than two-thirds that of the competing Focke-Wulf justified the selection of the Hs 129, and all proposals for production of the Fw 189C were abandoned.

FOCKE-WULF FW 189A

In the meantime, in the spring of 1940, Focke-Wulf had finally received production orders for the Fw 189A reconnaissance aircraft, and a pre-production batch of 10 **Fw 189A-0s** had

been followed on the Bremen assembly line by the initial production version, the **Fw 189A-1**, 20 examples of which had been completed by the end of the year when service evaluation was being undertaken by the *Aufklärungsstaffeln* (*H*). The favourable service reports, coupled with the OKL's acceptance of the obsolescence of the Hs 126A which had been underlined by combat attrition during the French campaign, led to high priority being allocated to Fw 189A production, and a second assembly line was established at the former Aero plant in Prague, Czechoslovakia.

Production tempo built up rapidly at Focke-Wulf's Bremen facility, but had begun to taper off during the early summer months owing to the plant's more urgent commitment to the Fw 190 fighter programme, and thus, while the parent company delivered only 99 Fw 189As during the course of 1941, the Aero plant delivered 151, and towards the end of the year the necessary jigs were delivered from Bremen to factories in the Bordeaux area for production of the Fw 189A to commence in France with final assembly being carried out at Mérignac.

The Fw 189A-1 was basically similar to the Fw 189 V4, apart from some additional aerodynamic refinement of the engine cowlings, the use of As 410A-1 standard units, twin-leg main undercarriage members, and minor changes in operational equipment. Armament was standardized on a pair of forward-firing MG 17 machine guns in the wing-roots and two MG 15 machine guns on flexible mountings, all of 7.9-mm. calibre, and four ETC 50/VIII racks were provided beneath the outboard wing panels for 110-lb. SC 50 bombs. One RB 20/30 camera was normally installed but optional installations were the RB 50/30, the RB 21/18 or the RB 15/18, and a hand-held HK 12.5 or HK 19 was usually carried. The crew comprised pilot, the navigator/radio-operator who doubled as bombardier and dorsal gunner, and the flight mechanic who doubled as rear gunner. The Fw 189A-1 was succeeded on the assembly lines in mid-1941 by the **Fw 189A-2** which differed solely in having strengthened defensive armament, this comprising MG 81Z (twin MG 81) machine gun installations in both the dorsal position and the cone of the fuselage nacelle. Manufactured in parallel

(Above and below) The Fw 189 V6, the prototype for the Fw 189C assault model, with abbreviated and heavily armoured central nacelle

An early production Fw 189A-1 under test near Bremen in the summer of 1941. The Fw 189A-2 differed only in having increased defensive armament

was the **Fw 189A-3** dual-control pilot trainer which was delivered to the *Luftwaffe* in small numbers, these being supplemented by a number of Fw 189A-0 and A-1 aircraft modified to similar standards.

The first Fw 189A-0 aircraft had been delivered to a training *Staffel*, 9.(H)/LG 2, in the autumn of 1940, this unit earlier having received several of the Fw 189B trainers during the previous spring, but when the assault on the Soviet Union began on June 22, 1941, all the operational *Aufklärungsstaffeln* (*H*) were still equipped with the Henschel Hs 126. However, by the end of 1941, units were being progressively withdrawn for re-equipment, and in the spring of 1942 substantial numbers of Fw 189A-1s and A-2s were appearing in the ranks of the *Aufklärungsstaffeln* (*H*) and their successors, the *Nahaufklärungsgruppen,* on the Russian front where the type was to serve almost exclusively.

The year 1942 saw a marked increase in production deliveries of the Fw 189A, despite the fact that the manufacture of this type was

steadily tapering off at the Bremen plant where only 57 machines were built. The Aero plant produced 183 machines, but the principal reason for the increased deliveries was the phasing in of the Bordeaux group of factories which delivered 87 Fw 189As during the course of 1942, the Mérignac plant attaining an assembly rate of 20 machines per month in September of that year. By the spring of 1943, the French factories were to be the sole source of Fw 189A supply, the Bremen and Prague factories finally phasing out production in the first two months of 1943 with 11 and 3 machines respectively, while 194 examples left the Mérignac assembly line which, with a further 12 machines produced during the first weeks of 1944, brought total production of the Fw 189A to 828 aircraft, excluding prototypes.

During 1942, a batch of 14 Fw 189A-1s was supplied to the Slovakian Air Force, and late in the year a quantity of Fw 189A-2s reached Hungary to equip the Hungarian 3/1 Short-Range Reconnaissance Squadron which was deployed in Russia from March 1943, saw extensive use in the summer offensive around

(Above and left) An Fw 189A-1 (SI-EG) with tropical finish. Only one Staffel employed this type in North Africa

Kharkov, and continuously undertook reconnaissance and light bombing sorties in support of the Hungarian forces until March 1944. In *Luftwaffe* service the Fw 189A had virtually completely supplanted the Hs 126A with the *Nahaufklärungsgruppen* on the Eastern Front by the end of 1942, and one *Staffel* with a mixture of Fw 189As and Bf 110Cs was operating in North Africa. In operational service, the Fw 189A surpassed all expectations, proving capable of undertaking sorties under the most adverse conditions and of absorbing considerable punishment yet still regaining its base. It was sufficiently agile to evade all but the most determined fighter attacks, and provided it possessed a well co-ordinated crew, its defensive armament was effective enough to deter even these. On occasions it survived Russian *Taran* or ramming attacks, returning to base with half the vertical tail surfaces missing.

The final A-series production model introduced onto the assembly lines late in 1942 was the **Fw 189A-4** which was intended to fulfil both tactical reconnaissance and close support tasks, two 20-mm. MG FF cannon supplanting the 7.9-mm. MG 17 machine guns in the wing roots, and light armour being added beneath the engine nacelles, fuel tanks and portions of the fuselage nacelle.

Consideration was given to producing a version of the Fw 189 powered by two Gnôme-Rhône 14M 4/5 14-cylinder radial air-cooled engines each rated at 700 h.p. for take-off, and one Fw 189A-1 airframe was actually converted to take these power plants after installation drawings had been prepared by the SNCASO drawing office at Chatillon-sur-Seine. It was proposed that the Gnôme-

(Above) An Fw 189A-2 (H1-IN) employed as a personal transport by Fieldmarshal Kesselring

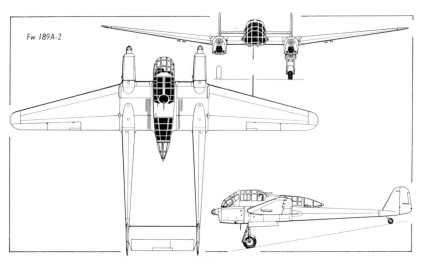

Fw 189A-2

An Fw 189A-2 of 1.(H)/31 which was serving on the Russian Front in the summer of 1942

Rhône-powered version be manufactured as the **Fw 189E**, but the prototype crashed in the vicinity of Nancy while being ferried to Germany for evaluation, and the entire scheme was abandoned.

Another more powerful version of the basic design was the **Fw 189F-1** which, employing a basic Fw 189A-2 airframe, was powered by a pair of Argus As 411MA-1 engines which, similar in general construction to the As 410A-1 but having a different gear ratio and increased r.p.m., offered 580 h.p. for take-off

and 600 h.p. at 2,000 ft. When assembly finally came to a halt at Mérignac in 1944, the Fw 189F-1 had just been phased onto the production line, and only 17 examples of this version were delivered to the *Luftwaffe*. A more radically modified development, the **Fw 189G** with 950 h.p. Argus As 402 engines and a number of structural changes, was planned for production in 1942, but in the event the As 402 engine failed to attain production status, necessitating the abandoning of this project.

FOCKE-WULF FW 189A-2 SPECIFICATION

Type: *Three-seat Tactical Reconnaissance and Army Co-operation aircraft.* **Power Plants:** *Two Argus As 410A-1 12-cylinder inverted-vee air-cooled engines each rated at 465 h.p. for take-off and 415 h.p. at 7,875 ft.* **Armament:** *Two 7.9-mm. MG 17 machine guns in wing roots, two 7.9-mm. MG 81 machine guns on flexible mounting in dorsal position, and two 7.9-mm. MG 81 machine guns in tail of fuselage nacelle, plus four 110-lb. SC 50 bombs on ETC 50/VIIId underwing racks.* **Performance:** *(At 8,708 lb.) Maximum speed, 217 m.p.h. at 7,875 ft.; maximum cruising speed, 202 m.p.h. at 7,875 ft.; economical cruising speed, 190 m.p.h.; normal range, 416 mls.; endurance, 2 hr. 10 min.; service ceiling, 23,950 ft.* **Weights:** *Empty, 6,239 lb.; empty equipped, 7,154 lb.; normal loaded, 8,708 lb.; maximum loaded, 9,193 lb.* **Dimensions:** *Span, 60 ft. 4½ in.; length, 39 ft. 5½ in.; height, 10 ft. 2 in.; wing area, 409.029 sq. ft.*

FOCKE-WULF FW 191

By mid-1939, the German aircraft industry had amassed sufficient experience with pressure cabins for flight at extreme altitudes for the *Technische Amt* of the RLM to issue a specification to selected aircraft manufacturers calling for a high-altitude bomber. This specification demanded an extremely advanced performance and a defensive armament of remotely-controlled gun barbettes. Known as the "Bomber B" the aircraft was to be of twin-engined configuration, its power plants being either Junkers Jumo 222s or Daimler-Benz DB 604s, both extremely advanced 24-

(Right and below) The Fw 191 V1 under test early in 1942

(Above) The Fw 191 V1 and (below) Fw 191 V2. Externally the two prototypes differed solely in that the latter had additional small windows immediately aft of the glazed nose

proposals to the *Technische Amt* in July 1940. The subsequent evaluation placed the Junkers Ju 288 and the Focke-Wulf Fw 191 as winning contenders, the Arado Ar 340 being eliminated and the Dornier Do 317 being shelved as a possible later back-up programme.

A Focke-Wulf team led by Dipl. Ing. Kosel began detail design of the **Fw 191** immediately, and as the intended Jumo 222 engines (selected in preference to the DB 604 which was destined to be finally abandoned in 1942) were obviously not going to be ready in time for installation in the first prototype airframes, it was agreed with the *Technische Amt* that these should be completed with BMW 801 air-cooled cylinder liquid-cooled engines at an early stage of development. One of the most important requirements was pressurized accommodation for a crew of three or four, and the specification was issued to Arado, Dornier, Focke-Wulf and Junkers who submitted their final radials which were then the most powerful engines available and were of generally similar size to the Junkers engine.

Construction of the first two prototypes, the **Fw 191 V1** and **V2**, began late in 1940, the first of these commencing its flight test programme early in 1942 with Dipl. Ing. Melhorn at the controls. The Fw 191 V2 joined the test programme shortly afterwards, the two aircraft being virtually identical apart from slight differences in cockpit glazing. The Fw 191 was an extremely clean all-metal shoulder-wing monoplane, following normal German practice in having all four members of the crew grouped together in the fuselage nose which it was intended to pressurize in the production model.

All fuel was housed by two cells in the wing centre section and a series of five cells in the fuselage above the bomb-bay, and both the V1 and V2 were fitted with mock-ups of the remotely-controlled defensive barbettes. These comprised a chin barbette intended to accommodate a pair of 7.9-mm. MG 81 machine guns and directed by the bombardier-navigator, two barbettes containing similar armament in the tails of the engine nacelles, and a dorsal barbette with a single 20-mm. MG 151 cannon and two MG 81s, all of which were to be directed by the radio-operator, and, lastly, a central barbette with one MG 151 and two MG 81s directed by the flight engineer.

One of the most unusual features of the Fw

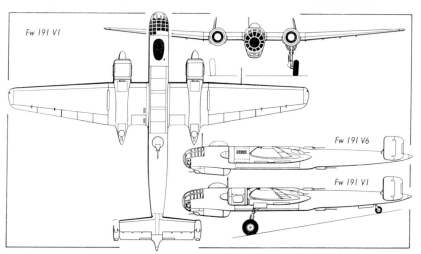

Fw 191 V1

Fw 191 V6

Fw 191 V1

191 was the use of electrics for all systems. Every safety device or trimming control, in fact, every item normally actuated mechanically or hydraulically was powered by an electric motor. Indeed, so numerous were the small electric motors that the aircraft was promptly dubbed the *Fliegende Kraftwerk*, or Flying Power Station! This extensive use of electrics had been made at the behest of the research department of the RLM, the *Forschungsabteilung*, despite protests from Focke-Wulf that such a concept was impracticable, involving an immense "electrical weight" and rendering the aircraft extremely vulnerable in combat—one bullet passing through the right place being sufficient to put the main systems and all communications out of action! As was anticipated, from the outset

of flight testing the electrical systems proved a constant source of trouble, a flight test rarely being completed without one or other system failing. Another source of trouble, but one less expected, was the ingenious *Multhopp-Klappe*, a combined landing flap and dive brake fitted in four sections to the wing trailing edges, and which, when extended, presented a severe flutter problem. These troubles were compounded by the fact that the aircraft was dangerously underpowered, its two BMW 801 MA 14-cylinder two-row radials each offering only 1,380 h.p. at 15,100 ft., and this for an aircraft weighing upwards of 45,000 lb. in test condition.

The Fw 191 V1 had completed a series of 10 flights when it was joined in the test programme by the Fw 191 V2, but progress was so

The Fw 191 V2 with the rear fuselage and tail of the Fw 191 V1 in the foreground. It will be noted that the radio mast of the V1 had been transferred aft to a position immediately ahead of the dorsal barbette

disappointing owing to the numerous teething troubles that, after the completion of 10 hours flying by the two prototypes, the flight test programme was halted. Simultaneously, further prototype construction was shelved pending the development of the electrical systems to an acceptable stage of reliability and the availability of more powerful engines.

Three additional prototypes had been ordered in the meantime, and, together with the Fw 191 V3, two of these airframes had reached an advanced stage of assembly. From the outset it had been intended that the production Fw 191A would receive the Junkers Jumo 222, and trial installations were planned for the Fw 191 V3, V4 and V5, but it had soon become obvious that this power plant would demand an appreciably longer gestatory period than had been envisaged when the "Bomber B" programme had been formulated. In fact, owing to the persistent and apparently insoluble teething troubles, doubts were being

expressed in some quarters that the Jumo 222 would ever achieve production status. Thus, by the end of 1941 proposals had been made to supplant the Jumo in the Fw 191A with either the DB 606 or the DB 610, these each comprising a pair of 12-cylinder DB 601 and DB 605 engines respectively, each pair of units being mounted side by side and driving a single airscrew through a common reduction gear. Although the Daimler-Benz engines were substantially larger and heavier than the Jumo 222, they were appreciably more advanced in development, and were looked upon as an interim solution pending availability of the Junkers power plant.

Dipl. Ing. Kosel had made repeated applications to the RLM for permission to replace the more troublesome electrical systems in the Fw 191 by hydraulic systems, and late in 1942, with the decision to install a pair of flight-cleared pre-production Jumo 222 engines in an Fw 191 for evaluation, permission was granted

---

FOCKE-WULF FW 191B SPECIFICATION

(This specification is based on manufacturer's estimates for the proposed production models with the DB 610 and, in parentheses, with the DB 606)

Type: *Four-seat Medium Bomber.* **Power Plants:** *Two Daimler-Benz DB 610A/B (DB 606) 24-cylinder liquid-cooled engines each rated at 2,870 (2,700) h.p. for take-off and 2,560 (2,650) h.p. at 25,000 (15,800) ft.* **Armament:** *One 20-mm. MG 151 cannon or two 12.7-mm. MG 131 machine guns in remotely-controlled nose barbette, two 20-mm. MG 151 cannon in each of dorsal and ventral barbettes, and either one 20-mm. MG 151 cannon or two 13-mm. MG 131 machine guns in extreme tail. (Offensive) Eight 550-lb. or four, 1,102-lb. bombs, or two 3,300-lb. LT 1500 torpedoes internally, plus (overload condition) two 1,102-lb. bombs or two LT 1500 torpedoes externally.* **Performance:** *Maximum speed, 352 (347) m.p.h. at 12,965 (13,720) ft., 393 (375) m.p.h. at 31,000 (30,800) ft.; range with 865 Imp. gal. fuel, 1,120 (1,180) mls. at 310 (291) m.p.h., with 1,665 Imp. gal., 2,400 (2,490) mls. at 304 (266) m.p.h.; initial climb rate at 52,600 (52,000) lb. 1,500 (1,320) ft./min.; service ceiling at 51,000 (50,800) lb., 28,800 (27,200) ft.* **Weights:** *Normal loaded, 52,600 (52,000) lb.; maximum overload, 55,800 (55,100) lb.* **Dimensions:** *Span, 85 ft. 3½ in.; length, 64 ft. 4¾ in.; height, 18 ft. 4½ in,; wing area, 758.855 sq. ft.*

A model of the Fw 191A bomber as originally proposed with Jumo 222 engines

to introduce hydraulics in place of electrics. The sixth prototype airframe, the **Fw 191 V6,** which was least advanced when the construction programme had been shelved, was selected for completion with hydraulic systems and Jumo 222 engines, and flew with these in the spring of 1943 with Focke-Wulf's chief test pilot, Flugkapitän Hans Sander, at the controls. The Jumo 222 engines each offered 2,200 h.p. for take-off, but flight test results with the Fw 191 V6 still left much to be desired.

At this time it was proposed that the aircraft should be produced as the **Fw 191B** with either two DB 606 or DB 610 coupled power plants. Defensive armament had been revised to comprise a single 20-mm. MG 151 cannon in the chin barbette, twin MG 151 cannon in the dorsal and ventral barbettes, and a remotely-controlled 20-mm. MG 151 cannon or two 13-mm. MG 131 machine guns in the extreme tail, the engine nacelle barbettes having been deleted. Internal load could comprise either four 1,102-lb. bombs or two 3,300-lb. LT 1500 torpedoes, and this could be supplemented by two 1,102-lb. bombs, two LT 1500 torpedoes, or two LMA III para-chute sea mines on underwing racks between the fuselage and the engine nacelles. Parallel proposals were made for what was, in effect, a simplified version of the basic design with pressure cabin and the complex system of remotely-controlled gun barbettes deleted in favour of manually-operated guns and manned hydraulically-operated gun turrets. Known as the **Fw 191C,**

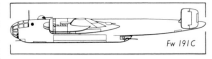

Fw 191C

this was to have had four separate power plants, these being Jumo 211Fs, DB 601Es, DB 605s or DB 628s, a deeper bomb-bay and more minor changes. However, after limited flight testing at Delmenhorst, the Fw 191 V6 had been transferred to Wenzendorf where it arrived simultaneously with the RLM's announcement of its decision to abandon the entire "Bomber B" programme. Thus, before the end of 1943, all work on the Fw 191 terminated, and neither the Fw 191B nor Fw 191C left the drawing board.

FOCKE-WULF FW 200 CONDOR   GERMANY

Forced upon Germany by circumstances against which her leaders had gambled, the Focke-Wulf Fw 200 Condor maritime reconnaissance-bomber was an improvisation, having been designed solely as a commercial transport, but such was its success as a commerce raider that it was to be referred to by Winston Churchill as the scourge of the Atlantic. The outcome of short-sightedness on the part of the *Oberkommando der Luftwaffe* (OKL) and the *Oberbefehlshaber*, Hermann Göring, though the Condor reconnaissance bomber may have been, it demanded an inordinate effort on the part of the Allies before its threat was finally nullified, and by that time it had been responsible for sinking an immense tonnage of Allied shipping. Despite little more than a respectable endurance

(Above and below) The Fw 200 V1 photographed during initial flight trials late in July 1937. This aircraft was subsequently registered D-AERE and named Saarland

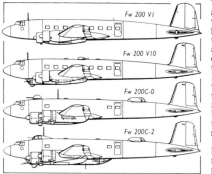

Fw 200 V1

Fw 200 V10

Fw 200C-0

Fw 200C-2

to commend it, in its heyday the Condor, co-operating with U-boat packs, posed a major threat to Britain's survival.

The Condor stemmed from discussions held in the spring of 1936 between Focke-Wulf's Technical Director, Prof.Dipl.Ing. Kurt Tank and Lufthansa's Director, Dr. Stüssel, during which Tank propounded his concept of four-engined airliner utilizing wings of relatively high aspect ratio and capable of transatlantic operation. Design and the construction of a fuselage mock-up continued throughout the early summer months, and in mid-July Lufthansa placed a development contract with Focke-Wulf for what had by now become the Fw 200 Condor (the RLM-allocated type number being considerably higher than those being applied to new aircraft types at that time but one considered by Tank to be ideally suited for publicity purposes).

Some indication of Tank's certainty of the basic soundness of the Condor's design is revealed by the fact that construction of three prototypes began in the autumn of 1936 in parallel with preparations for a pre-production batch of nine aircraft. The first prototype, the **Fw 200 V1**, subsequently registered D-AERE and named *Saarland*, flew on July 27, 1937, mere 12 months and 11 days from the date on which Lufthansa had signed the contract.

The Fw 200 V3 completed as the official Führermaschine for the personal use of Adolf Hitler

An Fw 200B-2 taken over by the Luftwaffe while still on the Focke-Wulf assembly line and subsequently used by K.Gr.z.b.V.105

Powered by four Pratt & Whitney Hornet S1E-G nine-cylinder radial air-cooled engines each rated at 875 h.p. for take-off, the Fw 200 V1 demanded only some minor redesign of the vertical tail surfaces as a result of initial flight trials, and was quickly joined in the development programme by the **Fw 200 V2** D-AETA *Westfalen*) and the **Fw 200 V3** D-2600 *Immelmann III*), the latter being designated the official *Führermaschine* for the personal use of Adolf Hitler and his retinue, and one of two Condors ordered by the *Reichsluftfahrtministerium* (RLM) for governmental use. The second and third aircraft were essentially similar to the Fw 200 V1 apart from having BMW 132G-1 (licence-built Pratt & Whitney Hornet) engines each having a normal rating of 720 h.p.

Subsequent aircraft, which began to leave Focke-Wulf's Bremen assembly line in the spring of 1937, were designated as **Fw 200A-0** pre-production machines, although the majority of them were also to be allocated *Versuchs* numbers. For example, the Fw 200A-01 (*Werk-Nr.* 2893) D-ADHR *Saarland*

(this fleet name being transferred from the Fw 200 V1 when that aircraft was renamed *Brandenburg* in the summer of 1938) was also designated **Fw 200 V4**, while the Fw 200A-03 (D-AMHC *Nordmark*) was the **Fw 200 V5**. The second A-series pre-production aircraft, the Fw 200A-02 (*Werk-Nr.* 2894), had in the meantime been purchased by Det Danske Luftfartselskab (DDL) which began operating commercial services with this machine (as OY-DAM *Dania*) in July 1938, the Danish airline later acquiring the Fw 200A-05 (*Werk-Nr.* 2993) as OY-DEM *Jutlandia*.

The Fw 200A-04 (D-ACVH *Grenzmark*) and Fw 200A-06 (D-ARHW *Friesland*) fitted with BMW 132L engines were also known as the **Fw 200 V6** and **V7** respectively, while the Fw 200A-07, initially flown as D-ASBK, was delivered to the Brazilian Sindicato Condor Limitada (as PP-CBJ *Arumani*), together with the Fw 200A-08 (PP-CBI *Abaitara*), and the final A-series Condor, the Fw 200A-09 (alias **V9**) was delivered to Lufthansa in the summer of 1939 as D-AXFO *Pommern*.

While production of the airliner was being

The first of four Fw 200C-0 transports (Werk-Nr. 021) completed as D-ASVX Thüringen in January 1940 but taken over by the Luftwaffe

established, the Condor had undertaken a series of long-distance publicity flights, the first of these, from Berlin to Cairo with one intermediate stop at Salonica, being flown by the Fw 200 V4 (D-ADHR) on June 27, 1938. A further long-distance flight began on August 10, 1938, when the Fw 200 V1 took off for a non-stop flight from Berlin to New York. For this flight the Fw 200 V1 was redesignated **Fw 200S-1** (the "S" suffix letter indicating *Sonder* or Special), was renamed *Brandenburg* and was allocated the special registration D-ACON. The aircraft covered the 4,075 miles against strong headwinds in 24 hr. 55 min. at an average speed of 164 m.p.h. The return journey was effected in 19 hr. 47 min. at an average speed of 205 m.p.h. over a slightly more southerly route.

On November 28, 1938, the Fw 200S-1 D-ACON took off for Tokyo, stopping at Basra, Karachi and Hanoi for refuelling, and arriving at the Japanese capital in slightly less than 48 hours elapsed time of which 42 hr. 18 min. was spent in the air. On the return flight, however, a fuel shortage resulted in the aircraft being ditched in shallow water off Manila.

By the autumn of 1938, work had begun on what was considered to be the initial production model, the Fw 200B, which, with minor structural modifications, was proposed in two versions; as the **Fw 200B-1** with the BMW 132Dc engines each rated at 850 h.p. at 8,200 ft., and as the **Fw 200B-2** with BMW 132H engines rated at 830 h.p. at 3,600 ft. By comparison with the Fw 200A-0, the Fw 200B-1 had empty and normal loaded weights increased from 21,560 lb. and 32,120 lb. to 24,860 lb. and 38,500 lb. respectively. Structurally similar, the Fw 200B-2 possessed a slightly higher empty weight at 24,912 lb., but normal loaded weight was lower at 37,479 lb.

Japanese interest in the Condor had been aroused by the visit of D-ACON to Tokyo, and early in 1939, the Dai Nippon Kabushiki Kaisha, or Japan-Manchuria Aviation Company, signed a contract for five Fw 200Bs, this order being rapidly followed by a contract from the Finnish airline, Aero O/Y, for two Fw 200B Condors. The Japanese contract for five transports was accompanied by a supplementary contract, but this, placed on behalf of the Imperial Japanese Navy, received no publicity as it called for a single example of the Fw 200B adapted for the long-range maritime reconnaissance role. At the time this contract was received by Focke-Wulf the prototype B-series airframe, the **Fw 200 V10**, was already under construction, and Tank elected to adapt this aircraft to fulfil the Japanese reconnaissance requirement. The Fw 200 V10 was therefore actually preceded into the air by several of the Fw 200B transports being built against the Japanese and Finnish contracts.

In the event, the last Condors to be exported were the two Fw 200A-0 aircraft for Brazil delivered in August 1939, as by the time the first B-series aircraft were ready for delivery hostilities had begun in Europe and permission for their export was withheld, several of the aircraft being added to Lufthansa's fleet, the sole Fw 200B-1 becoming D-ASBR *Holstein*, and a trio of Fw 200B-2s becoming D-ABOD *Kurmark*, D-AMHL *Pommern* (as a replacement for D-AXFO which had been written off), and D-ASHH *Hessen*.

The Condor's service with Lufthansa was destined to be strictly limited, and at no time were more than four aircraft of this type to be included on the airline's fleet strength. When World War II began, Lufthansa was operating the Fw 200 V4 (D-ADHR), V5 (D-AMHC), V7 (D-ARHW) and V9 (D-AXFO). The Fw 200 V6 (D-ACVH), which had been used by Ribbentrop when he flew to meet Stalin in Moscow in the summer of 1939, and the Fw 200 V3 (*Immelmann III*) were held in the transport reserve pool at Berlin-Tempelhof, these being the only two Condors on *Luftwaffe* strength when World War II began.

During the winter of 1939–40, Lufthansa's Condor fleet was briefly supplemented by the four Fw 200Bs but in the following spring was once more depleted when most of the Condors were taken over by the *Luftwaffe* as part of the equipment of a special purposes transport unit, K.Gr.z.b.V. 105, which, in April 1940, was based at Kiel-Holtenau for the logistic support of German forces engaged in the invasion of Norway. Subsequently, two of the Fw 200Bs were returned to Lufthansa which operated these alongside the Fw 200 V4 (D-ADHR) and V5 (D-AMHC) until 1941 when the V4 was written off together with one of the Fw 200Bs (D-ABOD), reducing the airline's Condor fleet to two aircraft. In 1943, the loss of the Fw 200 V5 reduced the fleet to one Condor, and this, the Fw 200B-2 D-ASHH, had the distinction of operating Lufthansa's last wartime scheduled flight on April 14, 1945, flying from Barcelona to Berlin.

(*Above, left and at foot of opposite page) Early production Fw 200C- Condor maritime recon naissance bombers pro duced at Cottbus ir 1940*

D-ASHH was lost a week later when, on April 21st., it was hastily loaded with the baggage of the Berlin Headquarters Staff, and took-off for Barcelona, via Munich, the pilot *Flugkapitän* Künstle, being confident of evading Allied fighters in view of the prevailing bad weather. The aircraft reached Munich safely, took-off again and disappeared.

Enquiries in Germany, Switzerland and Spair continued for a number of years, but it wa not until 1954 that the mystery was finall; solved when evidence was found near Piesen kofen Kreis Mühlberg, Bavaria, that th heavily-loaded Condor had crashed an(burned out with no survivors. Only on commercial German-registered Condor sur

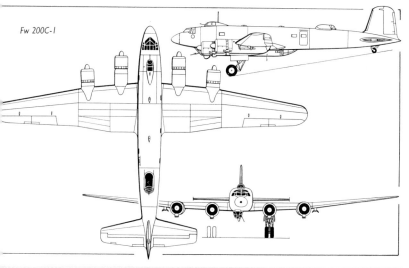

Fw 200C-1

vived until the end of the war, this being the Fw 200B-2 D-AMHL *Pommern* which, originally built against the Japanese order, had been operated by the so-called *Viermotorige Transportstaffel* and its successor, *Lufttransportstaffel* 290, under the direct command of the *Lufttransport-Chef Berlin*.

FOCKE-WULF FW 200C

Work on the adaptation of the Fw 200 V10 to meet the Japanese maritime reconnaissance requirement was still in progress whe
hostilities began in Europe. The airframe wa
little changed from that of the standard F
200B transport, but a single 7.9-mm. MG 1
machine gun was mounted in a dorsal turr
positioned slightly forward of the wing trailin
edge, and a short ventral gondola was mounte
offset to starboard beneath the forwar
fuselage, this housing the observer's static
and single hand-operated MG 15 machin
guns firing fore and aft. Much of the fusela
was occupied by fu
tanks, and two vertic
cameras were attache
to the floor of th
centre fuselage wit
the camera operate
seated aft.

The *Oberkomman
der Luftwaffe* ha

*(Left) An Fw 200C-2
KG 40, and (below)
Fw 200C-1 prior
delivery*

(Above and right) Fw 200C-3/U1 Condors with the large hydraulically-operated HDL 151 forward turret

gambled on having the Heinkel He 177 available for the long-range reconnaissance and anti-shipping roles, and when hostilities actually commenced belatedly awoke to the *Luftwaffe*'s total lack of an aircraft possessing sufficient range to harass British shipping far out in the Atlantic. The He 177 was still very much an unknown quantity as prototype trials had still to be initiated, and the *Reichsluftfahrtministerium* (RLM) was urgently requested to investigate the possibility of adapting the Condor for interim *Luftwaffe* use as a maritime reconnaissance-bomber pending production of the He 177. As a four-engined commercial transport carrying four crew members and 26 passengers, the Condor employed a relatively light structure hardly suited for the military role now envisaged, but drawing upon its experience in adapting the Fw 200 V10 to meet Japanese requirements, the Focke-Wulf team drew up a proposal for a modified version, the **Fw 200C**, which was promptly accepted by the RLM and preparations initiated for an assembly line at Cottbus.

In essence, the airframe of the Fw 200C remained unchanged from that of the Fw 200B, apart from some minor local strengthening, and the BMW 132H engines of the Fw 200B-2 were retained, but some refinement of the engine nacelles was accompanied by the introduction of long-chord engine cowlings, and to accept the higher weights at which the military model was intended to operate the single mainwheels were supplanted by twin-wheel units. A pre-production batch of 10 **Fw 200C-0** Condors was ordered in September 1939 from the Bremen plant for delivery while the Cottbus factory was tooling for the production **Fw 200C-1**, and these pre-production aircraft were, in fact, Fw 200B airframes already on the assembly line when war began. The first four airframes were too advanced to be adapted for the maritime reconnaissance role and were therefore completed as transports without defensive armament, although the new twin-wheel main undercarriage members, modified engine nacelles, long-chord cowlings and three-blade variable-pitch airscrews were fitted. The first of the four Fw 200C-0 transports (*Werk-Nr.* 021) was completed in January 1940 as D-ASVX *Thüringen*, and it was intended to deliver this aircraft to Lufthansa. However, before it could be taken over by the airline, the aircraft was sequestered by the *Luftwaffe* (as NA-WN) and, together with the three following aircraft, was delivered to K.Gr.z.b.V. 105 for transport operations during the Norwegian invasion.

The remaining six Fw 200C-0 Condors were completed with defensive armament and bomb racks for anti-shipping operations, and during the early spring of 1940 were delivered to the 1.*Staffel* of the newly formed I *Gruppe* of *Kampfgeschwader* 40 which began attacks on British shipping from Danish bases in April. By May 11, 1940, only two of the Fw 200C-0

Condors of I/KG 40 were serviceable, and by the end of June, 1.*Staffel* had been withdrawn from operations for re-equipment with the Fw 200C-1 and transferred to Bordeaux-Merignac where it was attached to the *IV Fliegerkorps* under *Luftflotte* 3 for operations in support of the attack on the British Isles. Flying out across the Bay of Biscay and following an arc around Eire's Atlantic coastline, attacking targets of opportunity, and landing at Trondheim-Vaernes or Stavanger-Sola in Norway, I/KG 40 enjoyed some success although it suffered losses, one Condor being shot down over the Channel on July 13th and another North of Ireland on July 20th. By September 1940, prior to which the unit had undertaken some nocturnal bombing in the Liverpool-Birkenhead area, Condor strength had risen to 15 aircraft, and a *Geschwader Stab* had been established, although this possessed only one Condor. During August-September, I/KG 40 accounted for more than 90,000 tons of Allied shipping, but one of its most spectacular successes was the discovery and bombing of the 42,348-ton Canadian Pacific liner *Empress of Britain* some 70 miles North-West of Donegal Bay on October 26th, the crippled liner being taken in tow but torpedoed and sunk two days later by the U-32.

Whereas the Fw 200C-0 possessed a defensive armament comprising one 7.9-mm. MG 15 machine gun in an hydraulically-operated upper turret immediately aft of the flight deck, a similar weapon on a flexible mounting firing from a raised aft dorsal position, and a third MG 15 firing aft and downward through a ventral hatch, the Cottbus-built Fw 200C-1 introduced a long ventral gondola offset to starboard, the nose of which accommodated a 20-mm. MG FF (Oerlikon) cannon on a flexible mounting, the tail of the gondola mounting an MG 15 which supplanted the weapon fired through the ventral hatch. A

*An Fw 200C-3/U2 (SG-KS) with Lotfe 7D bomb sight in nose of ventral gondola, this neces-
sitating the replacement of the 20-mm. MG 151 by a 13-mm. MG 131*

further change was provided by the deletion of
the hydraulically-operated forward turret and
its replacement by a fixed raised cupola which,
also accommodating a single MG 15 on a
flexible mounting, was, unlike the ventral
gondola, centred on the fuselage.

The offensive load for armed reconnaissance
missions was similar for both the Fw 200C-0
and C-1, this comprising a single 551·lb.
bomb under each of the extended outboard
engine nacelles and a further 551-lb. bomb
on each of two underwing racks immediately
outboard of the engines, but the ventral
gondola of the Fw 200C-1 included provision
for the stowage of a single 551-lb. cement
bomb which was used as a marker for checking
the accuracy of bombsight readings and for
assisting final adjustments before dropping
the four H.E. bombs.

The Fw 200C featured a semi-monocoque
fuselage with an all-metal, two-spar wing
built in three sections, metal covered to the
rear spar and fabric covered aft. Two-piece
ailerons extended along two-thirds of the
outer section trailing edges, and split flaps
were mounted inboard of the ailerons. The
Fw 200C-1 normally carried a crew of five
which comprised pilot, co-pilot, navigator/
radio-operator/gunner, engineer/gunner and
rear dorsal gunner. As the Condor was
intended primarily for low-altitude attack, the
navigator, who also fulfilled the function of
bombardier, had to rely on a Revi sight. The
basic fuel tankage totalled 1,773 Imp. gal.
but an overload of 198 Imp. gal. could be
carried in an armoured auxiliary tank in the
ventral gondola, and on occasions this overload was increased even further for maximum
endurance unarmed reconnaissance missions
by the addition of two or three 66 Imp. gal.
drums which were stowed in the fuselage and
used to refill the tanks in flight.

Twenty-six Fw 200C-1 Condors had left the
Cottbus assembly line by the end of 1940, and
Gruppe strength was gradually built up,
although attrition was relatively high as a
result of the aircraft's commercial transport
heritage rather than combat. Only the first
pilot of the Condor enjoyed any armour
protection and, all fuel connections to the

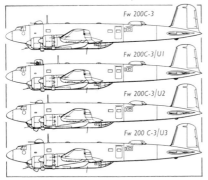

Fw 200C-3

Fw 200C-3/U1

Fw 200C-3/U2

Fw 200 C-3/U3

engines being on the underside of the aircraft, it was extremely vulnerable to light anti-aircraft fire. However, the inadequate anti-aircraft armament of Allied merchant vessels at this stage of the war, coupled with insufficient escort vessels and almost complete lack of long-range aircraft and escort carriers rendered I/KG 40's task a relatively simple one. The "Achilles Heel" of I/KG 40's Condors was the haste with which they had been adapted for their task. Embodying virtually no structural strengthening they soon proved inadequate to meet the strain of continuous operational flying at low altitudes

(*Below*) *Fw 200C-3/U2 Condors at Cottbus prior to delivery to KG 40*

The Fw 200C-3/U2, like the original Fw 200C-3, had a low-drag Fw 19 hydraulically-operated forward turret but introduced a Lotfe 7D bomb sight

for long periods, and the violent manoeuvres that were sometimes called for when taking evasive action. There were numerous instances of the rear spar failing and the fuselage breaking its back immediately aft of the wing on landing, and during the latter half of 1940 rarely more than six–eight Condors were available for operations at any one time.

Despite its shortcomings, however, the Condor continued to enjoy auspicious success, and between August 1, 1940 and February 9, 1941, I/KG 40 accounted for 85 Allied vessels totalling some 363,000 tons. By March 1941, when, as a result of the increasing importance of the sea war, the *Fliegerführer Atlantik* was established, I/KG 40 had become a full three-*Staffel Gruppe* with an operational strength of 36 Condors, although the average *Gruppe* serviceability rate rarely exceeded 25 per cent of total strength. The Fw 200C-1 had been supplanted on the assembly line at Cottbus by the **Fw 200C-2** which was considered as an interim model pending the introduction of the more extensively modified Fw 200C-3. The Fw 200C-2, like its production predecessor, was BMW 132H-powered, and differed in having

new scalloped outboard engine nacelles which offered some drag reduction when their racks were loaded with either a 551-lb. bomb or a 66 Imp. gal. auxiliary fuel tank. New faired wing racks were also introduced, but these changes did not reduce the essential vulnerability of the Condor, and by the late summer of 1941 the offensive operations of the Condor had to be curtailed by the *Fliegerführer Atlantik* owing to rising combat attrition.

The effectiveness of the anti-aircraft defences of Allied merchant vessels had been steadily increased and catapult-launched fighters had made their début. Thus, Condor crews received orders not to initiate any attack and to seek cloud cover when attacked, only offering fight if absolutely necessary. Further, they had orders to return immediately to base even if only slightly damaged rather than continue to operate and jeopardise the safety of a valuable aircraft, their task being largely confined to shadowing Allied convoys. On sighting the convoy the Condor's crew informed its base, the aircraft's captain giving his opinion as to whether the convoy could best be dealt with by U-boats or by bombers. If it was decided to attack the convoy with

U-boats, the Condor sometimes acted as the U-boats' *Fühlungshalter*, or contact plane, by sending out continuous D/F signals, its tactics being controlled by the *Befehlshaber der U-Boote* (Flag Officer Submarines), no direct communication taking place between the aircraft and the submarines that it was responsible for directing.

By the summer of 1941, the improved **Fw 200C-3** began to reach KG 40, this embodying major structural strengthening of both the rear spar and the fuselage, although the Condor was still to suffer structural failures, and the Focke-Wulf concern never succeeded in entirely eradicating the problem. In order to maintain the performance of the Condor despite the substantially increased structural and equipment weights, the Fw 200C-3 received four BMW-Bramo 323R-2 Fafnir nine-cylinder radials which, rated at 1,000 h.p. at sea level, offered 1,200 h.p. for take-off by means of methanol-water injection. Loaded weight had risen to 46,297 lb., an additional crew member was carried, and maximum bomb load was increased to 4,626 lb. (comprising one 1,102-lb. bomb beneath each outboard engine nacelle, one 551-lb. bomb on each of the two underwing racks, and 12 110-lb. bombs in the ventral gondola),

(Above) The 20-mm. MG FF in the ventral gondola of an Fw 200C-3, and (below) an Fw 200C-3 on a compass swinging platform

FOCKE-WULF FW 200C-3/U4 CONDOR SPECIFICATION

Type: *Seven-seat long-range Maritime Reconnaissance-Bomber.* **Power Plants:** *Four BMW-Bramo 323 R-2 Fafnir nine-cylinder radial air-cooled engines each rated at 1,200 h.p. for take-off with methanol-water injection, 1,000 h.p. at sea level and 940 h.p. at 13,120 ft.* **Armament:** *(Defensive) One 7.9-mm. MG 15 machine gun with 1,000 rounds in hydraulically-operated Fw 19 forward dorsal turret, one 13-mm. MG 131 machine gun with 500 rounds on flexible mounting in aft dorsal position, two 13-mm. MG 131 machine guns with 300 r.p.g. firing from aft beam hatches, one 20-mm. MG 151 cannon on flexible mounting with 500 rounds in forward ventral position, and one 7.9-mm. MG 15 machine gun on flexible mounting in aft ventral position. (Offensive) Maximum bomb load of 4,626 lb. comprising two 1,102-lb., two 551-lb., and 12 110-lb. bombs.* **Performance:** *Maximum speed, 224 m.p.h. at 15,750 ft., 190 m.p.h. at sea level; maximum cruising speed, 208 m.p.h. at 13,120 ft., 172 m.p.h. at sea level; economical cruising speed, 158 m.p.h.; range at economical cruising speed (with standard fuel—1,773 Imp. gal.), 2,210 mls., (with 2,190 Imp. gal.), 2,760 mls.; service ceiling, 19,000 ft.* **Weights:** *Empty, 28,550 lb.; maximum loaded, 50,045 lb.* **Dimensions:** *Span, 107 ft. 9½ in.; length, 76 ft. 11½ in.; height, 20 ft. 8 in.; wing area, 1,290 sq. ft.*

although, in effect, such a load was never to be carried for the offensive reconnaissance mission for which bomb load was invariably restricted to the quartette of 551-lb. bombs.

A low-drag Fw 19 hydraulically-operated turret with a single 7.9-mm. MG 15 machine gun replaced the central raised fairing immediately aft of the flight deck, and two additional MG 15s were mounted behind sliding beam panels. The **Fw 200C-3/U1** differed in having a large hydraulically-operated HDL 151 forward turret housing a single 15-mm. MG 151 cannon with a 500-round belt and a spare 300-round belt, and a 20-mm. MG 151 cannon with a 300-round belt in the nose of the ventral gondola in place of the old Fw MG FF. Although the HDL 151 turret provided an appreciably more effective defence than the Fw 19 with its 7.9-mm. weapon, its drag was not inconsiderable, reducing maximum speed by 16–18 m.p.h., and the **Fw 200C-3/U2** reverted to the Fw 19 forward turret. The primary change in the Fw 200C-3/U2 was the

introduction of the Lotfe 7D bomb sight which necessitated the replacement of the 20-mm. MG 151 cannon in the nose of the ventral gondola by a 13-mm. MG 131 machine gun as the breach of the cannon interfered with the bomb sight's stowage. The Lotfe 7D substantially improved the Condor's bombing accuracy, and it was claimed that the average error was only 20–30 yards from a release altitude of 10,000–13,000 ft. The **Fw 200C-3/U3** had an EDL 131 forward turret with a 13-mm. MG 131 machine gun and a similar weapon on a flexible mounting in the aft dorsal position, while the **Fw 200C-3/U4**, which carried an additional gunner to bring the crew complement to seven, and increased fuel capacity which boosted maximum loaded weight to 50,045 lb., retained the Fw 19 forward turret but mounted 13-mm. MG 131 weapons in place of the 7.9-mm. MG 15s in the beam positions.

Total Condor production during 1941 was only 58 machines, despite increased demand

for the aircraft as a result of delays in the introduction of the He 177. Bomb damage to the Cottbus facility was partially responsible for delivery delays, this having necessitated the transfer of much final assembly work on the Condor to one of the Blohm und Voss plants. Indeed, deliveries could barely keep pace with I/KG 40's demands, and although the re-

equipment of III/KG 40 with the Condor was considered a matter of urgency, only a few of these aircraft had reached this *Gruppe* by the end of 1941, and immediately an aircraft came off the line a KG 40 crew was specially sent to Cottbus to collect it. The shortage of Condors was further aggravated by the diversion of aircraft for special transport duties with the *Reichskurierstaffel*.

In February 1942, production of the Fw 200C-3 gave place to the **C-4**, this model being destined to be manufactured in larger numbers than any other Condor variant. The C-3 and C-4 were basically similar aircraft, the principal differences being confined to those associated with search radar and communications radio. Early production Fw 200C-4s were fitted with FuG *Rostock* search radar with antennae on the fuselage nose and above and below the outboard wing panels, but Condors soon standardised on the later FuG 200 *Hohentwiel* which was used in conjunction with a blind bombing procedure, the *Rostock* serving solely for shipping search. A few of the aircraft of *Stab III/KG 40* were later fitted with both *Hohentwiel* and *Rostock*, the double installation being necessitated by the fact that the latter, although having a wider search angle and a greater range than the former, would not provide readings at a range of less than three miles and was therefore unsuitable for blind bombing, the *Hohentwiel* being accurate down to a range of less than a mile.

The large HDL 151 turret was restored on the Fw 200C-4, and either a 13-mm. MG 131 or 20-mm. MG 151 was mounted in the nose of the ventral gondola, according to whether the Lotfe 7D bomb sight was carried, all other defensive positions mounting 7.9-mm. MG 15 machine guns. The rated altitude of the Fw 200C-4 was 15,750 ft. at which maximum speed was 205 m.p.h. as compared with 224 m.p.h. at the same altitude for the Fw 200C-3. At sea level the average cruising speed was 150–168 m.p.h., maximum speed being 174 m.p.h., and service ceiling was officially

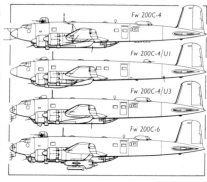

19,000 ft., but at this altitude the airframe was subject to violent vibration. The standard tankage provided a normal endurance of 14 hr. at economical cruise with normal safety

One of the two special transport versions of the Fw 200C-4, the C-4/U1 (Werk-Nr. 137), with abbreviated ventral gondola and accommodation for 11 passengers

The second of the two special transport conversions of the Fw 200C-4, the C-4/U2 (Werk-Nr. 138), with accommodation for 14 passengers

reserves, but endurance could be stretched to 18 hr. with overload fuel.

The Allies, who had begun to take the measure of the Condor with the introduction of CAM-ships, enjoyed further successes with the appearance of the very-long-range Liberators of R.A.F. Coastal Command which effectively closed the Atlantic Gap, and with the introduction of escort carriers. Several Condors of KG 40 were lost in December 1941 to Wildcats from HMS *Audacity*, one of the first escort carriers to see operational service. Early in 1942, I/KG 40 was transferred to Trondheim-Vaernes in Norway to engage Russian-bound shipping under *Luftflotte* 5, III/KG 40 continuing to operate primarily from Bordeaux-Mérignac from where, towards the end of the year, 9.*Staffel* was detached for transport tasks from Lecce in southern Italy.

During 1942, a total of 84 Fw 200C-3 and C-4 Condors was produced, a few of these being delivered to the Ju 88-equipped 1.(F)/120 based in Norway, and the similarly equipped 1.(F)/122 based in Sardinia, but the bulk of the Condors were still absorbed by KG 40 as they became available. However, at the beginning of 1943, Condor activity over the Atlantic fell sharply, 2./KG 40 remaining at Trondheim-Vaernes but 1. and 3./KG 40 being despatched to Russia for emergency transport operations. The two *Staffeln*, with an operational strength totalling 18 aircraft, began ferrying supplies into the beleaguered German garrison at Stalingrad, and were known as the *Sonder-Unternehmung Stalingrad*, or K.Gr.z.b. V.200. Initially the Condors landed supplies on an airfield on the outskirts of Stalingrad, but as the German perimeter shrank they were forced to drop supplies by parachute, each aircraft carrying four supply containers on its bomb racks. On January 18, 1943, the Condors of K.Gr.z.b.V.200 were transferred from Stalino to Zaparozhe from where they continued their supply-dropping activities for a month before it was decided that this transport undertaking was too costly. For five days the Condors then confined their activities to bombing railway communications in the Stalingrad area, after which the survivors were withdrawn to Berlin-Staaken where they became 8./KG 40 (new 1 and 3 *Staffeln*

82

having been formed in the meantime on He 177s), this unit then transferring to Bordeaux-Mérignac for a resumption of activities over the Bay of Biscay. In the meantime, 7.*Staffel*, which had also been sent to Italy on a transport assignment, and 9.*Staffel* had returned to France, being based at Cognac and Bordeaux-Mérignac respectively, and once again the Condor began to appear in numbers.

Production of the Condor continued throughout 1943, a total of 76 aircraft being delivered in that year, and these including a number of **Fw 200C-8**s built specifically as carriers for the Henschel Hs 293A missile. Prior to the delivery of the Fw 200C-8s late in

1943, a small number of Fw 200C-3/U1 and U2 Condors were adapted to carry the Hs 293A, these being known after modification as **Fw 200C-6**s. Equipped with the FuG 203b *Kehl III* transmitter for use with the FuG 230b *Strassburg* receiver of the Hs 293, the Fw 200C-6 carried a pair of these missiles on

(*Above and below*) *An Fw 200C-8 (Werk-Nr. 256) with FuG 200 Hohentwiel radar array. The Fw 200C-8 was the last sub-type of the Condor to be built*

special carriers beneath the outboard engine nacelles. The Fw 200C-6 was used operationally by III/KG 40 for the first time on December 28, 1943, when one of four of the *Gruppe*'s Condors engaged in a search for British naval units carried two Hs 293A missiles. In the event, the operation was abortive, as the Hs 293-carrying Condor encountered a patrolling Sunderland before it could make contact with the British vessels, and was forced down with the missiles still unlaunched. The last few production Condors were Fw 200C-8s, those examples intended specifically for the Hs 293-launching role having deeper outboard engine nacelles and a forward-extended ventral gondola, the final eight aircraft being completed in January–February 1944, but by that time the Condor's days as an anti-shipping aircraft were numbered, and with the loss of KG 40's bases on the Biscay coast one of the two surviving III/KG 40 Condor *Staffeln* was transferred to Norway and the other withdrawn to Germany.

From mid-1944, the Condor was being employed increasingly and not inappropriately in the role for which it had been originally designed—that of transportation. Two special transport versions of the Condor had, in fact, been built in 1942, these being the **Fw 200-4/U1** (*Werk-Nr.*137) and the **Fw 200-4/U2** (*Werk-Nr.*138) featuring an abbreviated ventral gondola, an Fw 19 forward upper turret and a generally similar Fw 20 aft dorsal turret, both mounting a single 7.9-mm. MG 15 machine gun, and similar weapons in the nose and tail of the gondola. The two aircraft differed solely in seating arrangements, the Fw 200C-4/U1 providing accommodation for 11 passengers and the Fw 200C-4/U2 accommodating 14. After the disbanding of KG 40 in the autumn of 1944, 8./KG 40 was redesignated *Transportstaffel Condor*, and three ex-KG 40 Condors were passed to *Transportstaffel 5* in December 1944, these subsequently being transferred to the *Oberkommando Süd-Ost* at Vienna.

OPERATIONAL METHODS

Reference has already been made to the vulnerability of the Condor owing to its lack

An Fw 200C-8/U10 (Werk-Nr. 259) with deepened outboard nacelles for Hs 293 missiles

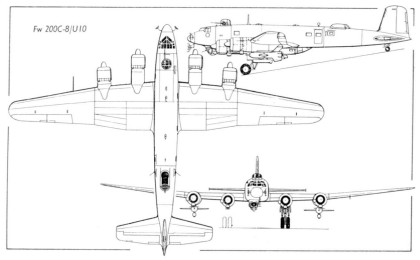

Fw 200C-8/U10

of armour and the fact that all fuel lines were on the underside of the aircraft, and as the danger of interception by long-range patrolling Beaufighters and Mosquitos increased, the most northerly point to which Biscay-based Condors flew was 40° N, there thus being no longer any link between the Biscay area and the northern waters patrolled by the Norwegian-based Condor *Gruppe* by 1942. There were two main areas of armed reconnaissance patrol operated by III/KG 40 Condors based on Cognac and Bordeaux-Mérignac, one known as the *Kleine Aufklärung*, or limited reconnaissance, and the other known as the *Grosse Aufklärung*, or extended reconnaissance.

The dividing line between the two reconnaissance areas was approximately 45°, the smaller extending to the limit already mentioned, and the larger to approximately 34° N. The westerly limit of both areas was normally 19° N, although on special reconnaissances Condors reached as far as 25° W.

When approaching the northerly reconnaissance area, the Condors normally flew in formation at sea level for mutual protection, breaking up and proceeding singly on their shipping search at 11° W. Sometimes Condors en route for this area had to make a detour as far South as Cap Ortegal to avoid patrolling fighters. One method of shipping search

frequently adopted was known as the *Fächer* (Fan), a typical search of this type in a southerly direction starting from 15° W was to fly due West for 3°, due South for 30 miles, due East for 3°, due South for 30 miles, and so on until the allotted area had been covered.

With the return of the Condors from emergency transport operations in Russia and Italy in the spring of 1943, III/KG 40 operating from Cognac and Bordeaux-Mérignac discontinued its previous practice of flying routine reconnaissance in search of shipping targets, these duties being taken over by the Ju 290As of FAGr 5 based at Mont de Marsan. In concert with the He 177s of II/KG 40 and the similarly-equipped 1 and 3 *Staffeln* of I/KG 40, the Fw 200s became solely concerned with shipping attack, being sent on a sortie only when a definite target had been sighted and its position reported.

The departures of Allied convoys from Gibraltar were regularly reported from Spain, and the time of arrival of the convoy in KG

40's sphere of operations could therefore be calculated, and it only remained for FAGr 5 to establish the exact position of the convoy and weather conditions in the area before the Condors and He 177s took-off. The only exception to this new policy was when the total effort of all aircraft in the Biscay area was demanded by the *Fliegerführer Atlantik*, such as when German blockade runners were attempting to make port. On such occasions the Condors reverted to armed reconnaissance to report the presence of any Allied warships in the area.

When Allied shipping was reported, a minimum of four Condors would take off to attack, the aircraft usually flying at sea level in close formation to a point such as Cap Ortegal before fanning out and flying on parallel courses at intervals of 25–30 miles. Each aircraft would periodically climb to 1,500 ft. in a wide circle, making a search with its *Hohentwiel*, after which the original course was resumed. The first Condor to sight the shipping would then make R/T contact with the other aircraft. Low-level attack in conditions of clear visibility was expressly forbidden, a minimum attacking altitude of 9,000 ft. being prescribed.

Whereas the aircraft based in the Biscay area were concerned with shipping attack, the Condors based on Trondheim-Vaernes were engaged almost entirely on unarmed reconnaissance, shipping sightings merely being reported back to base, and bombing attacks were not normally performed by Condors in northern water. A typical patrol from Trondheim-Vaernes called for a direct course to the N.E. coast of Iceland and Jan Mayen Island before returning to base, or to the northern coast of Iceland and thence to a point some 40 miles from the coast of Greenland before returning. The normal daily effort from Trondheim-Vaernes was only one aircraft.

As a warplane the Condor was not a particularly outstanding aircraft, but in view of the relatively small number of Condors available for operations at any one time it established a formidable record in the two years during which it could truly be referred to as the "Scourge of the Atlantic".

The Condor was plagued with structural failures throughout its service career, and the photographs (above right and below) illustrate Fw 200C-3s of KG 40 after suffering rear spar and aft fuselage failures

HEINKEL HE 46 GERMANY

When the 'thirties dawned, the *Luftwaffe* already existed in embryo, and the *Reichswehr* Ministry was encouraging the small but industrious German aircraft industry to develop new combat aircraft for this clandestine fledgeling. Among the most active of the German aircraft manufacturers was the Ernest Heinkel Flugzeugwerke at Warnemünde, which, at the behest of the *Reichswehr*, began the development in 1931 of two new warplanes, the He 45 light tactical bomber and the He 46 army co-operation and tactical reconnaissance aircraft.

At this time, the biplane configuration was widely considered to be obligatory for most types of military aircraft and, accordingly, both the He 45 and He 46 were biplanes, but although parallel developments of generally similar overall size, no commonality of structure or design feature existed between them. Whereas the He 45 was an orthodox unequal-span staggered biplane powered by a 12-cylinder liquid-cooled BMW VI engine, the lighter He 46 was a true sesquiplane with marked sweep on the upper mainplane and a Siemens-built Bristol Jupiter nine-cylinder air-cooled radial. Both aircraft were to be ordered into production in substantial quantities, but while the He 45 was to make its journey down the assembly lines virtually unchanged, the He 46 was transformed from biplane to monoplane configuration at a very early stage in its development.

The first prototype of the He 46, the He 46a, was flown for the first time late in 1931, displaying pleasant flying characteristics and the demanded docility of handling. However, the lower mainplane blanketed a consider-

(*Left*) *An He 46E-1 (circa 1937) with the observer utilizing the supplementary hand-operated camera*

88

Twenty He 46C-1s were supplied to the Spanish Nationalist forces for operation by Grupo 3-G-11, and examples of this type are seen above and right in service in Spain

able portion of the observer's downward view and the decision was taken to delete the lower wing, compensating for this by extending the upper wing from 37 ft. 8¾ in. to 45 ft. 11¼ in. With these modifications flight testing was resumed early in 1932, by which time the He 46a had been joined by the similarly-powered **He 46b** which, like its predecessor, performed its initial trials in biplane configuration. Despite some loss in gross wing area, the handling characteristics of the He 46a as a monoplane were little changed from those experienced during flight testing as a biplane, and apart from a somewhat too leisurely performance which it was decided to rectify by substituting a Siemens SAM 22B nine-cylinder radial rated at 660 h.p. for take-off in

place of the lower-powered Jupiter, the aircraft fully met the requirements of the *Reichswehr*.

A third prototype, the **He 46c**, was completed, this embodying all the progressive modifications introduced on the first two machines, together with full military equip-

(*Left*) *An He 46E-2 in the winter of* 1938–39

Gothaer Waggon-fabrik at Gotha and the Fieseler Flugzeugwerke at Kassel each contributed 24 and 12 He 46s, although during 1933–34, the bulk of production was undertaken at Warnemünde where 200 examples were produced, plus the three prototypes.

In 1936, when defiance of the restrictions imposed by the various treaties signed after World War One was becoming fashionable, the Bulgarian government decided to establish a nucleus of an air arm in contravention of the Treaty of Neuilly, and purchased 18 **He 46C-2** reconnaissance aircraft from Germany, these differing from the *Luftwaffe's* He 46C-1 solely in having an NACA-type engine cowling. The Hungarian government followed suit by ordering a batch of the improved **He 46E-2** model which also featured the NACA cowling but introduced improved radio equipment and a modified camera installation.

ment, including defensive armament of a single 7.9-mm. MG 15 machine gun on a ring in the rear cockpit, and in 1933 large-scale production was begun for the short-range *Aufklärungsstaffeln* of the future *Luftwaffe*. Powered by the SAM 322B radial, the initial production model was designated **He 46C-1** and featured a bay beneath the observer's cockpit which could house a single Zeiss camera or a maximum of 20 22-lb. bombs in vertical racks.

The new production programme for military aircraft initiated by Erhard Milch on January 1, 1934, which provided for the manufacture of 4,021 aircraft of all types by September 30, 1935, demanded substantially more He 45s and He 46s than could be produced by the existing Heinkel facility at Warnemünde, necessitating an extensive sub-contracting programme for both types, the principal subcontractors for the He 46 being the Siebel Flugzeugwerke at Halle and the MIAG plant at Leipzig which respectively built 159 and 83 He 46s, while the

Prior to the appearance of the E-series, minor changes in the He 46C-1 had resulted in the D-series which entered production at Warnemünde after the delivery of six preproduction **He 46D-0** aircraft (each of which was allocated a civil registration: D-IJIA, D-ITEU, D-ITAI, D-ILUO, D-IXUI and D-IRAN). The first production **He 46D-1** (D-ILHE) was later fitted with an NACA engine cowling as the **He 46e** prototype for the definitive **He 46e** production model, the **E-1**,

E-2 and E-3 differing in the type of radio and other equipment installed, but most being delivered to the *Luftwaffe*'s *Aufklärungsstaffeln (H)* without the engine cowling fitted to the prototype, despite the fact that this added 16 m.p.h. to maximum speed. One He 46C airframe was fitted with a cowled 14-cylinder Armstrong Siddeley Panther engine of 560 h.p. as the **He 46f** trainer, and 14 production **He 46F-1** and **F-2** trainers were produced for the training *Staffeln*.

By 1936, when production of the He 46 was finally phased out, the type was standard *Luftwaffe* short-range reconnaissance and army co-operation equipment. Twenty He 46C-1s were delivered to the Spanish Nationalists in September 1936, these being dubbed *Pavas* in Spanish service and, in April 1937, equipping

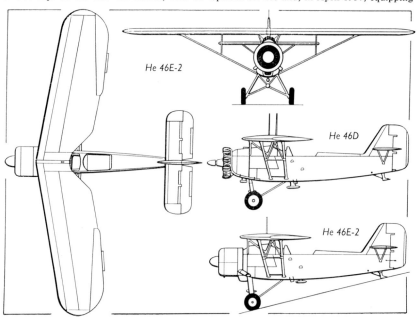

He 46E-2

He 46D

He 46E-2

the three squadrons of *Grupo* 3-G-11, finally being relegated to the training role with the *Escuela de Observadores* at Malaga in August 1938.

Replacement of the He 46 in the *Aufklärungsstaffeln* (*H*) began in the spring of 1938 with the delivery of the first Henschel Hs 126A-1s, but with the beginning of September 1939 and the commencement of hostilities, five *Staffeln* were still completely equipped with the He 46, these being 4.(H)/12 with *Luftflotte* 2 in North-West Germany, 2.(H)/23 and 4.(H)/23 with *Luftflotte* 3 in Southern Germany, and 2.(H)/31 and 4.(H)/31 with *Luftflotte* 4 in South-West Germany, Czechoslovakia and Austria, those *Staffeln* with the last-mentioned *Luftflotte* seeing action in Poland. Several other *Aufklärungsstaffeln* (*H*) included examples of the He 46 on their strength. However, the Hs 126 had entirely supplanted the He 46 in first-line *Luftwaffe* units in time for the invasion of France and the Low Countries in May 1940, although the *Aufklärungsstaffel Oberost* still possessed eight He 46s on strength.

All *Aufklärungsstaffeln* (*H*) participating in the attack on the Soviet Union were equipped with the Hs 126, but in the South the Hungarian Air Force's contingent accompanying the Hungarian Army's Fast Corps in Russia included the 1 Short-Range Reconnaissance Squadron equipped with He 46E-2, although few operations were flown as the unit was constantly moving from airfield to airfield in the wake of the advancing Hungarian troops. In the summer of 1942, the 3/2 Short-Range Reconnaissance Squadron with 12 He 46E-2s on strength arrived in Russia, and after a short spell of tactical reconnaissance switched to bombing operations. The 3/2 Squadron remained on operations until replaced by the Fw 189s of the 3/1 Squadron in March 1943, surprisingly losing only one of the elderly Heinkels to enemy action and accounting for three Soviet fighters.

In the spring of 1943, shortly after the withdrawal of the Hungarian He 46s from the Russian Front, the so-called *Störkampfstaffeln*, which had been established to emulate Russian tactics with slow, obsolete aircraft for nocturnal harassing, were assembled into *Nachtschlachtgruppen*, and He 46s withdrawn from training schools were included on their strength alongside various other elderly types. Initially, the He 46s carried 22-lb. bombs in their internal bay but as these proved extremely vulnerable to ground fire they were replaced by drop containers accommodating 110-154 lb. of small incendiary or fragmentation bombs which were dropped from altitudes between 800 and 3,300 feet.

HEINKEL HE 46D-1 SPECIFICATION

Type: *Two-seat Tactical Reconnaissance and Army Co-operation Aircraft.* **Power Plant:** *One Bramo* (*Siemens*) *SAM 322B nine-cylinder radial air-cooled engine rated at 650 h.p. for take-off and 580 h.p. at 3,280 ft.* **Armament:** *One 7.9-mm. MG 15 machine gun on flexible mounting in rear cockpit and (optional) 20 22-lb. bombs internally.* **Performance:** *Maximum speed, 155 m.p.h. at sea level, 161 m.p.h. at 2,625 ft.; cruising speed, 130 m.p.h. at sea level, 137 m.p.h. at 2,625 ft.; normal range, 497 mls. at 6,560 ft.; maximum range, 650 mls.; climb to 3,280 ft., 2.6 min., to 6,560 ft., 5.5 min.; ceiling, 19,685 ft.* **Weights:** *Empty, 3,230 lb.; empty equipped, 3,890 lb.; loaded, 5,070 lb.* **Dimensions:** *Span, 45 ft. 11¼ in.; length, 31 ft. 2 in.; height, 11 ft. 1¾ in.; wing area, 346.598 sq. ft.*

During the opening phases of World War II the Heinkel He 111 was undoubtedly a formidable offensive weapon. An elegant, well-built, efficient aircraft with good flying characteristics, it was a thoroughbred, inheriting its shapely contours from its single-engined predecessor, the He 70 Blitz, and temporarily placing Germany in the forefront of medium bomber development. The He 111 was to suffer the misfortune, however, of being forced to soldier on long past its allotted span owing to the inability of the German aircraft industry to produce a suitable replacement. Indeed, it was already approaching obsolescence when called upon to carry the major burden of the *Luftwaffe's* bombing offensive against the British Isles, and despite continuous modification and improvement it lacked the necessary stretch to keep pace with the rapidly changing requirements of the air war.

Like so many other German warplanes of its era, the He 111 was first revealed to the world in civil guise, and when demonstrated to the Press for the first time on January 10, 1936, at Tempelhof, Berlin, the He 111 V4 displayed was, indeed, the prototype for a 10-passenger commercial aircraft, but its slender, beautifully streamlined fuselage and low-drag elliptical wing were obviously designed for maximum performance, passenger comfort evidently being a very secondary consideration, and from the viewpoint of commercial operation its economics were, to say the least, questionable. Passenger accommodation was extremely cramped, a forward compartment between the wing spars providing seating for four passengers and a further compartment aft of the rear spar accommodating six passengers, and the aircraft's more lethal intent could be assumed.

What was *not* publicly revealed on that January morning in 1936 was the fact that the first prototype, which had flown nearly a year

The He 111a (later designated He 111 V1) was flown for the first time on February 24, 1935 with 660 h.p. BMW VI 6.0Z 12-cylinder engines

earlier, had been built as a bomber. Nor was it discovered that the first pre-production models of the bomber variant had already started down the assembly line at Rostock-Marienehe. It was subsequently to be claimed that the conception of the He 111 had been inspired by a specification issued by Deutsche Lufthansa for a high-speed transport offering greater capacity than the single-engined He 70, but the designers of the aircraft, Siegfried and Walter Günter, were aware from the outset that any order obtained from DLH would be limited and that the development of a machine suited only for the civil role would hardly be an attractive commercial proposition. Thus, the He 111 was designed as a dual-purpose aircraft; one that would be suitable for use as

a bomber by the still-clandestine *Luftwaffe* and as a transport by the DLH. Design emphasis was, however, placed on military potentiality, the planned rebirth of German military power suggesting that the *Luftwaffe* would present the most fruitful market in the years immediately ahead.

Design development of the new aircraft was initiated by the Günter brothers early in 1934, and the first prototype, the **He 111a**, was completed and rolled out of the assembly hangar at Marienehe for its first test flight on February 24, 1935. The initial flight test programme was in the charge of Gerhard Nitschke, and revealed the fact that flying characteristics were markedly superior to those of the He 70. Structurally, it was an orthodox cantilever low-wing monoplane of metal stressed-skin construction, and aerodynamically it was fully representative of the latest refinements in the state of the art. The long, slim nose terminated in a glazed cone for the bombardier, a traversing slot in the cone providing for the installation of a single 7.9-mm. machine gun, and it was proposed to mount similar weapons in an open dorsal position and a retractable "dustbin" ventral turret. Offensive armament was to comprise a 2,200-lb. load of bombs stowed vertically, and power was provided by a pair of BMW VI 6.0Z 12-cylinder liquid-cooled engines each offering a maximum output of 660 h.p. and a normal output of 500 h.p. Weighing 12,764 lb. empty and 16,755 lb. in normal loaded condition, the He 111a clocked 217 m.p.h. in level flight during its initial flight test phase, a speed closely comparable with those attained by contemporary fighters. Service ceiling was 17,720 ft., and maximum range was 930 miles.

Built in parallel with the first prototype were two further prototypes, the first of these, the **He 111 V2** (the initial aircraft having, in the meantime, been redesignated **He 111 V1**), being rolled out 16 days after its predecessor, to be followed closely by the **He 111 V3**. The three prototypes, although possessing essentially similar fuselages, each featured a different wing. Whereas the wing planform of the He 111 V1 was truly elliptical, spanning 82 ft. 0¼ in. and possessing an area of 942.917 sq.ft., that of the He 111 V2 embodied reduced curvature on the trailing edge, a reduction in overall span to 75 ft. 5½ in. and an increase in gross area to 952.6 sq.ft., while the wing of the He 111 V3 was essentially similar to that of the V2 but the tips were more sharply curved to result in yet a further decrease in overall span to 74 ft. 1¾ in. with a gross area similar to that of the He 111 V1.

Apart from the changes in wing planform, the prototypes differed in other respects, the He 111 V2 (D-ALIX) being arranged as a commercial transport, the bomb-bay becoming the "smoking compartment" for four passengers, provision being made for a further passenger compartment aft of the rear spar and a mail compartment being provided in the extreme nose. This aircraft was later delivered to DLH and, named *Rostock*, was used on some sectors of the South Atlantic mail service. The He 111 V3 (D-ALES) was the second bomber prototype and, apart from the wing and a slight increase in gross weight to 16,976 lb., was similar to the V1. It was, in fact, the production prototype for the He 111A series bomber, manufacture of a pre-production series of which was to be authorised later in 1935.

In the meantime, Heinkel proceeded with construction of the first true prototype for the commercial model, the **He 111 V4** (D-AHAO *Dresden*), which embodied results of the initial flight testing of the earlier prototypes. Powered by similar BMW VI 6.0Z engines driving three-blade variable-pitch airscrews (the V1 and V3 having two-blade adjustable pitch airscrews), the He 111 V4 possessed a similar wing to that of the V2, including the rather deeper fillets at the junctions of the wings with the fuselage that had characterised the second prototype airframe, and was fully equipped as a 10-passenger commercial transport. Intended as the production prototype for the He 111C series, the V4 flew late in 1935 and was subsequently delivered to DLH for route proving, being relinquished by the airline in 1937 and passed to the *Kommando* Rowehl (or the *z.b.V.Staffen beim RLM*), together with the He 111C-03 (D-AXAV *Köln*). Operating directly under the orders of Hermann Göring and commanded by *Oberstleutnant* Theodore Rowehl, this was a special

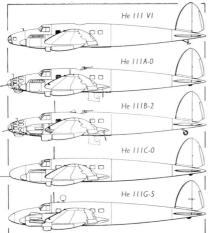

He III VI

He III A-0

He III B-2

He III C-0

He III G-5

machines for service evaluation. This pre-production batch comprised 10 He 111A-0 bombers which, based on the He 111 V3, differed from the prototype primarily in having an extended, more extensively glazed fuselage nose which increased overall length from 56 ft. 1¼ in. to 57 ft. 5in. The BMW VI 6.0Z engines drove three-blade variable-pitch airscrews, defensive armament comprised three 7.9-mm. MG 15 machine guns distributed between the glazed nose, the dorsal position and the retractable ventral "dustbin", and maximum bomb load was 2,205 lb., but gross weight had risen from the 16,976 lb. of the He 111 V3 to 18,122 lb., with the result that the bomber was seriously underpowered.

The He 111A-02 and -03 were delivered to Rechlin for official trials during the early spring of 1936, and the reports of the test pilots were distinctly discouraging. While unladen the He 111A possessed the pleasant handling characteristics of the prototypes, with full military load it became unresponsive and sluggish; at the most favourable altitude at full power and with the ventral "dustbin" retracted it could barely reach 192 m.p.h. in level flight, and its maximum cruising speed of 168 m.p.h. hardly represented a startling advance over existing bombers. The He 111A was promptly rejected as unsuitable for service with the *Luftwaffe*.

This decision was not unexpected by Heinkel, who had already initiated the flight testing of the very much more powerful He **111 V5**, a fact of which the *Reichsluftfahrtministerium* (RLM) was well aware, and he had already entertained a Chinese purchasing mission at Marienehe with a view to selling the He 111A to the government of Chiang Kai-shek which, in view of the rapid deterioration in Sino-Japanese relations, was most anxious to obtain modern bombers. The RLM's permission was sought to export the

photographic reconnaissance unit whose aircraft, bearing civil registrations and ostensibly engaged in route-proving, performed clandestine photographic sorties over British, French and Soviet territory. The He 111 V2 (D-ALIX *Rostock*) was later also passed to the *Kommando* Rowehl and, in fact, crashed during one of these clandestine missions, but its secret was not revealed.

HEINKEL HE 111A

From the outset of design development official interest had been displayed in the potentialities of the He 111 as a bomber for the future *Luftwaffe*, and late in 1935, Ernst Heinkel was instructed to proceed with the construction of a pre-production batch of

The He 111 V5 was the first DB 600A-powered prototype and was the predecessor of the He 111B series of bomber

bombers, and this being promptly granted, all 10 He 111A-0 aircraft were stripped of the standard *Luftwaffe* bomb sight, radio equipment and self-destroying charge, were disassembled and shipped to Canton.

HEINKEL HE 111B

Until 1935, German airframe manufacturers had suffered one serious handicap—the lack of a really high-powered liquid-cooled engine suitable for use by warplanes. The début of the Daimler-Benz DB 600A 12-cylinder inverted-vee liquid-cooled engine offering 1,000 h.p. for take-off was therefore greeted with particular enthusiasm, and Heinkel lost no time in obtaining two pre-production examples of the new power plant for experimental installation in an He 111 airframe.

The first DB 600A-powered aircraft, the He 111 V5 (D-APYS), possessed an identical airframe to the He 111A-0, and was rolled out at Marienehe early in 1936. The prototype for the proposed He 111B series, the V5 immediately displayed an appreciably better performance than any comparable bomber extant. Although gross weight had risen to 18,960 lb., maximum

speed was 224 m.p.h., while maximum cruising speed was 211 m.p.h. with full military load. It was as a result of the highly successful results obtained from the He 111 V5 that Heinkel evinced no disappointment when, several months later, the He 111A-0 was rejected for the *Luftwaffe*, as quantity production of the He 111B series had already been ordered, the pre-production batch of He 111As having only been ordered to provide the Heinkel plant with experience in manufacturing this advanced airframe pending the availability in quantity of the DB 600 engine. In fact, the RLM had already issued orders that a new plant specifically for He 111 production should be erected at Oranienburg.

The pre-production **He 111B-0,** which differed little from the He 111A-0 apart from its engines, followed the earlier model on the Marienehe assembly line, and the first examples of this bomber reached Rechlin in the autumn of 1936, where, apart from some aileron reversal at certain speeds, a defect that was quickly remedied, and the re-positioning of some items of service equipment, the aircraft was cleared for *Luftwaffe* service in a re-

(*Above and left*) *He 111B-1 bombers at Marienehe in the late autumn of 1936 prior to delivery to the Luftwaffe*

markably short time, deliveries of the **He 111B-1** to *Kampfgeschwader* 154 "Boelcke" (later redesignated KG 27) at Hannover-Langenhagen commencing during the early winter months.

The He 111B-1 had a loaded weight of 20,536 lb., and while the first few aircraft off the assembly line were powered by the DB 600Aa engine, subsequent aircraft standardised on the lower-rated DB 600C offering 880 h.p. for take-off and 850 h.p. at 13,120 ft.

The *Luftwaffe* was in no doubts as to its new bomber being second to none in capability, but the High Command was anxious to evaluate the aircraft under realistic combat conditions, and the conflict in Spain, presented an ideal opportunity to achieve both this and the evolution of suitable operational tactics. It was decided, therefore, to re-equip two *Staffeln* of the Condor Legion's bombing element, *Kampfgruppe* 88, with the He 111B-1, the first of 30 bombers of this type reaching Spain in February 1937, performing their first operational sortie on March 9th with an attack on the Republican airfields at Alcalá and Barajas. At the end of the same month, the He 111B-1 *Staffeln* joined with the main Spanish operational unit, the *Agrupación Española*, and the Italian *Aviacion Legionaria* in attacks on the Bilboa "iron belt", enjoying considerable success, the high performance of the Heinkel bombers enabling them to elude most opposing fighters.

The maximum short-range bomb load of the He 111B-1 had been increased to 3,307 lb., and the relatively light defensive armament of three MG 15 machine guns was generally considered by the Condor Legion to be adequate for the type of fighter opposition being encountered over Spain. The ventral "dustbin", which was occupied by the radio-operator, was only lowered over enemy territory and even then only when Republican fighters were in the vicinity as its drag had a serious effect on performance. Marienehe production of the He 111B was supplemented in May 1937 by the first deliveries from the new Oranienburg factory, both plants now manufacturing an improved sub-type, the **He 111B-2**. The He 111B-2 differed from the

-1 in having fully-supercharged DB 600CG engines rated at 950 h.p. for take-off and 910 h.p. at 13,120 ft. To overcome inadequate cooling experienced with the He 111B-1, the B-2 introduced supplementary surface coolant radiators on each side of the engines beneath the wing leading edges, and this version of the bomber followed the B-1 into service with *Kampfgeschwader* 154 which, by the late autumn of 1937, comprised Stab/KG 154 and I/KG 154 at Hannover-Langenhagen, II/KG 154 at Wunstorf and III/KG 154 at Delmenhorst, each *Gruppe* consisting of three 12-aircraft *Staffeln*.

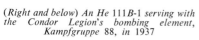

(*Right and below*) *An He 111B-1 serving with the Condor Legion's bombing element, Kampfgruppe 88, in 1937*

HEINKEL HE 111B-2 SPECIFICATION

Type: *Four-seat Medium Bomber.* **Power Plants:** *Two Daimler-Benz DB 600CG 12-cylinder liquid-cooled inverted-vee engines each rated at 950 h.p. for take-off and 910 h.p. at 13,120 ft,* **Armament:** *(Defensive) One 7.9-mm. MG 15 machine gun on spherical mounting in glazed nose, one 7.9-mm. MG 15 on flexible mounting in open dorsal position, and one 7.9-mm. MG 15 machine gun in retractable ventral "dustbin". (Offensive) Maximum bomb load of 3,307 lb. Typical bomb load comprising eight 220-lb. SC 100 bombs stowed nose up in individual cells.* **Performance:** *Maximum speed, 186 m.p.h. at sea level, 230 m.p.h. at 13,120 ft., 217 m.p.h. at 19,685 ft.; maximum cruising speed, 174 m.p.h. at sea level, 214 m.p.h. at 13,120 ft., 202 m.p.h. at 19,685 ft.; maximum range (with 1,653-lb. bomb load), 1,030 mls., (with 3,307-lb bomb load), 565 mls.; service ceiling, 22,966 ft.* **Weights:** *Empty equipped, 12,875 lb.; normal loaded, 18,960 lb.; maximum loaded, 22,046 lb.* **Dimensions:** *Span, 74 ft. 1¾ in.; length, 57 ft. 5 in.; height, 14 ft. 5¼ in.; wing area, 942.917 sq. ft.*

(Left) An He 111B-2 after a belly landing during wartime second-line service

HEINKEL HE 111C AND HE 111G

Despite Heinkel's preoccupation with the development of the He 111 bomber, development of the commercial model for DLH had continued at Marienehe, and a pre-production batch of six **He 111C-0** 10-passenger transports began to leave the assembly line in the summer of 1936, these being the He 111C-01 (D-AMES *Nürnberg*), the He 111C-02 (D-AQYF *Leipzig*), the He 111C-03 (D-AXAV *Köln*), the He 111C-04 (D-ABYE *Königsberg*), the He 111C-05 (D-AQUA *Breslau*), and He 111C-06 (D-ATYL *Karlsruhe*). At the end of 1936, the DLH concluded that the He 111C was too expensive and was uneconomical for normal airline service, and thus procurement of additional aircraft could not be justified. Nevertheless, during the summer of 1937, DLH was operating the He 111C-0 on daily services over the Berlin-Hanover-Amsterdam, Berlin-Nuremberg-Munich, and Cologne-Dortmund-Berlin routes. The He 111C-01 and

-05 were used on some sectors of the South Atlantic feederline service, together with the He 111 V2.

Although the six He 111C-0 transports were the only examples of the Heinkel design built against a DLH order, the German airline was eventually to receive four other aircraft of this type. The elliptical wing which characterised all early He 111s, although attractive from the aesthetic viewpoint and aerodynamically efficient, left much to be desired from the production viewpoint, and a new wing of simplified construction and straight taper had been designed early in 1936 and applied to an He 111B-0 fuselage and flight tested as the He 111 V7. This new wing was also adopted for the next commercial model, the He 111G, the first of two pre-production examples of which was flown in July 1936. This, the He 111G-01 (D-AEQU), alias V12, was powered by two BMW VI 6.0Zu engines, as was also the He 111G-02 (D-AYKI), alias V13, and both of these aircraft were passed to DLH in 1938 as *Halle* and *Magdeburg*, replacing the He 111 V4 and He 111C-03 which had been transferred to the *Kommando* Rowehl in the previous year.

One of the limiting factors of the He 111 from the commercial viewpoint was its BMW VI power plant which was primarily a military engine and insufficiently powerful. Thus, the next two G-series airframes were equipped with more powerful nine-cylinder air-cooled radials, these being the He 111 V14 (D-ACBS) with 880 h.p. BMW 132Dc engines, and the V15 (D-ADCF) with BMW 132H-1 engines of 870 h.p. These aircraft were also known as He 111G-3s, and when finally passed to DLH in 1938 as *Augsburg* and *Dresden* they were referred to as He 111Ls in order to differentiate between these experimental radial-engined examples and BMW VI-powered examples.

Yet another G-series airframe was the He 111 V16 (D-ASAR) which, also known as the He 111G-4, was powered by two specially de-rated DB 600G engines each offering 900 h.p. for take-off. This aircraft was eventually used as a personal transport by Field Marshal Erhard Milch. These five experimental aircraft were followed by a production batch of four He 111G-5 transports which, powered by DB 600Ga engines rated at 950 h.p. for take-off, were sold to Turkey.

Immediately prior to the war, the DLH He 111s were being operated over a dozen routes, as well as on the Berlin-Danzig-Königsberg sectors of Deruluft's Berlin-Moscow service, but on September 1, 1939, the majority of DLH's Heinkels were taken over by the *Luftwaffe*, fitted with military radio and other equipment, and placed in service as liaison aircraft.

HEINKEL HE 111D

Throughout the early months of 1937, the Heinkel drawing offices were preoccupied with developing and refining the basic He 111 design in order to improve performance and efficiency, and as each new variant of the DB 600 engine was evolved by Daimler-Benz it was applied to the bomber. The appearance of the DB 600Ga offering full rated altitude power of 950 h.p. led to a decision to introduce this engine as a successor to the DB 600CG equipping the He 111B-2, and, accordingly, an He 111B-0 airframe was re-engined with the DB 600Ga as the He 111 V9 (D-AQOX). Intended as the prototype for the He 111D series, the V9 retained the drag-evoking supplementary surface radiators of the He 111B-2 as a temporary measure while a complete redesign of the cooling system was being undertaken.

The He 111 V9 began flight trials in the summer of 1937, and during the following

The He 111 V9 (above) was the prototype for the He 111D series but retained the He 111B-type wing radiators pending redesign of the cooling system. These radiators were dispensed with by the He 111D, and one of the few production He 111D-1s is illustrated below

autumn it was joined by the first pre-production **He 111D-0**. Much effort had been expended in cleaning up the engine installation of this new version of the bomber. The surface radiators had been suppressed, a substantially deeper radiator bath having been introduced beneath the engine itself, the individual exhaust stubs had been shrouded and led via collector tubes to a single ejector exhaust pipe on each side of the engine, and the lines of the cowling

itself had been refined. Despite an increase in normal loaded weight to 19,423 lb., the He 111D-0 displayed a quite dramatic increase in performance, 25 m.p.h. being added to the maximum speed at 13,120 ft. to raise this to 255 m.p.h., while in "battle" condition with the ventral "dustbin" lowered, maximum speed at 230 m.p.h. was the same as that of the He 111B-2 with "dustbin" retracted.

Plans were immediately laid to introduce the **He 111D-1** on the assembly lines at Heinkel's Marienehe and Oranienburg fac-

practicable, the RLM ordered the immediate cessation of He 111D-1 production in favour of the proposed Jumo-powered He 111E until such times as the supply of Daimler-Benz engines proved sufficient to meet all demands, and thus the He 111D-1 failed to attain service with the *Luftwaffe's Kampfgeschwader*, the few examples completed serving as test aircraft.

HEINKEL HE 111E

After preliminary trials with the Junkers Jumo 210Ga in an He 111B-0 airframe which had

(*Right*) *The He 111 V6, originally a B-0 air-frame, was flown with both Jumo 210Ga and Jumo 211A-1 engines*

tories, and at Dornier's Wismar plant, but by the time the first few He 111D-1 bombers appeared late in 1937, a major bottleneck in the supply of the Daimler-Benz engines seemed likely to jeopardise the entire He 111 production programme. The *Luftwaffe's* immense re-equipment and expansion programme had resulted in a demand for DB 600 engines far beyond that within Daimler-Benz's immediate capacity, and as priority in supply was now enjoyed by Messerschmitt for the Bf 109 and Bf 110 fighters, Heinkel had no re-course but to find alternative power plants for his bombers. Fortunately, Heinkel had fore-seen such an eventuality, and had already investigated the possibility of installing the new Junkers Jumo 12-cylinder inverted-vee engines in the He 111. This having proved

become the **He 111 V6** (D-AXOH), it was concluded that this power plant, rated at 700 h.p. at sea level and 730 h.p. at 3,280 ft., was inadequate for the He 111, and thus the air-craft was re-engined with Jumo 211A-1s, these larger power plants being rated at 1,000 h.p. for take-off and 960 h.p. at 4,920 ft. The He 111 V6 was later transferred to Junkers for use as a test-bed for variable-speed airscrews, the first true prototype of the He 111E being the **He 111 V10** (D-ALEQ), a converted He 111D-0 airframe.

Powered by Jumo 211A-1 engines, the pre-production **He 111E-0** bombers appeared in January 1938, and, apart from their power plants and semi-retractable radiators, they were identical to the He 111D-1, having, in fact, started down the assembly lines as D-series

The first true prototype for the He 111E series was the He 111 V10 (above)

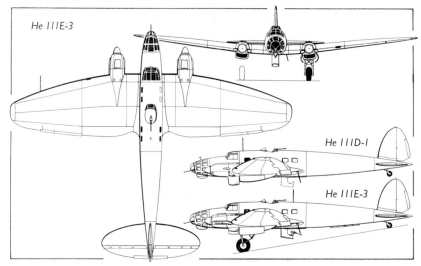

He 111E-3

He 111D-1

He 111E-3

airframes. Maximum bomb load was raised to 3,748 lb. and maximum permissible take-off weight to 22,720 lb., and for the production **He 111E-1** which followed in February 1938 maximum bomb load was further increased to 4,410 lb., maximum take-off weight rising to 23,370 lb.

In the meantime, the He 111B-1s operated by K/88 had enjoyed outstanding success during their first year of operation over Spain, and combat attrition had been remarkably low despite the technique of unescorted daylight sorties evolved by the two *Staffeln* equipped with the Heinkel bomber. It was decided, therefore, to equip all four of K/88's *Staffeln* with the He 111, and in March 1938 the first of 45 He 111E-1s reached Spain where they were soon emulating the success enjoyed by the earlier model. Throughout this period, the defensive armament of the He 111 had remained unchanged, and the comparatively light opposition encountered by K/88's He 111 *Staffeln* inclined the German High Command towards the erroneous belief that fast, un-escorted bombers with light defensive armament would continue to be able to operate with temerity in a hostile environment, a belief that was to cost the *Luftwaffe* dear over Britain a little more than two years later.

By the spring of 1938, the He 111 *Staffeln* of K/88 included a proportion of Spanish personnel which frequently formed mixed

(Below) An He 111E-1 photographed in February 1941 while serving with the Spanish air arm, and (above right) an He 111E-4 used for dropping trials with the L-10 torpedo

105

(Above) An He 111F-4 photographed at Vienna-Schwechat after relegation to the role of transport and courier aircraft

crews with members of the Condor Legion, and in August 1938, the He 111s were formed into the *Grupo* 10-G-25 at León. This unit continued to operate the He 111B-1s and E-1s until hostilities finally terminated when the *Grupo* was based on Logroño with the 58 surviving examples of the 75 He 111s sent to Spain. The He 111s remained in Spain, subsequently equipping the 14th and 15th Regiments based at Logroño and Zaragoza respectively, a few He 111B-1s and E-1s surviving in Spanish service until the end of the 'fifties.

At an early stage in the production of the He 111E, changes in equipment resulted in the E-1 being supplanted on the assembly line by the **E-3** sub-type which was to be manufactured in larger quantities than any other E-series bomber variant, this finally giving place to the **E-4** and **E-5**, neither of which was built in large numbers. Whereas the He 111E-3, like the E-1, carried its entire bomb load internally, the He 111E-4 featured electrically-actuated external fuselage bomb racks, and in maximum loaded condition

carried 2,205 lb. of bombs internally and a similar load externally. The He 111E-5 was basically similar to its predecessor but introduced as standard auxiliary fuel tanks with a total capacity of 183.5 Imp. gal. in the fuselage.

HEINKEL HE 111F

Early in 1936, the redesign of the He 111's wing had been initiated with the aim of simplifying the structure and eliminating the ellipses in order to ease manufacture, and the new straight-tapered wing, which possessed the same overall span and offered the same gross area as the elliptical wing that it supplanted, was first flown on a converted He 111B-0 airframe, the **He 111 V7**, during the summer of 1936. The new wing was adopted for the He 111G series of commercial transports, but although offering generally comparable efficiency to that of the elliptical wing and major reductions in cost and manufacturing time, it was not immediately accepted by the RLM's *Technische Amt* as its introduction on the assembly lines would have resulted in delivery delays which, during the

106

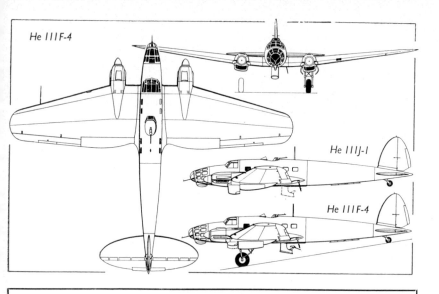

He 111F-4

He 111J-1

He 111F-4

HEINKEL HE 111E-3 SPECIFICATION

Type: *Four-seat Medium Bomber.* **Power Plants:** *Two Junkers Jumo* 211A-1 *12-cylinder liquid-cooled engines each rated at* 1,010 *h.p. for take-off and* 960 *h.p. at* 4,920 *ft.* **Armament:** *(Defensive) One* 7.9-mm. *MG* 15 *machine gun on spherical mounting in glazed nose, one* 7.9-mm. *MG* 15 *machine gun on flexible mounting in open dorsal position, and one* 7.9-mm. *MG* 15 *machine gun in retractable ventral "dustbin".* *(Offensive) Maximum of* 4,410 *lb. of bombs. Typical maximum load comprising eight* 551-*lb.* *SC* 250 *bombs suspended vertically in internal cells.* **Performance:** *Maximum speed,* 261 *m.p.h. at* 13,120 *ft.,* 218 *m.p.h. at sea level; maximum cruising speed,* 237 *m.p.h. at* 13,120 *ft.,* 202 *m.p.h. at sea level; maximum range (with* 2,205 *lb. bomb load),* 932 *mls.; service ceiling,* 23,620 *ft.* **Weights:** *Normal loaded,* 21,150 *lb.; maximum loaded,* 23,405 *lb.* **Dimensions:** *Span,* 74 *ft.* 1¾ *in.; length,* 57 *ft.* 5 *in.; height,* 14 *ft.* 5¼ *in.; wing area,* 942.917 *sq. ft.*

autumn of 1936, were considered to be best avoided. Thus, it was only during the following summer that serious consideration was given to standardising production on the new wing, the first bomber variant scheduled to embody this change being the He 111F.

To serve as a prototype for the F-series, an He 111B-1 was fitted with the new mainplanes, and retaining its DB 600CG engines was flown for the first time in July 1937 as the **He 111 V11.** Apart from having Jumo 211A-3 engines, which, offering 1,100 h.p. for take-off, were slightly more powerful than the A-1s of the He 111E, the pre-production **He 111F-0** which appeared late in 1937 differed in no major respect to the V11. Possessing a maximum loaded weight of 24,250 lb., it featured a similar fuselage fuel tank arrangement to that of the He 111E-5 which endowed it with a maximum range of 1,130 miles.

Early in 1938, the Turkish government began to evince interest in the Heinkel bomber, and after an He 111F-0 had been flown to Ankara for demonstration to the Turkish Air Force, protracted negotiations resulted in an order for 24 similar **He 111F-1** aircraft, deliveries of which began during the summer and were completed late in 1938, the aircraft equipping three bomber companies of the Turkish Air Force's 1st Regiment at Eskisehir and remaining in first-line service until 1946.

The He 111F-1 was not produced for the *Luftwaffe*, although a batch of 40 essentially similar **He 111F-4s** was delivered during the spring and summer of 1938, these differing from the bombers supplied to Turkey only in having similar internal and external bomb arrangements to those of the He 111E-4.

HEINKEL HE 111J

The situation regarding the supply of Daimler-Benz DB 600CG engines having eased slightly by the summer of 1938, Heinkel was instructed to install this power plant in another variant of the bomber which was manufactured in parallel with the He 111F-4, the He 111J. It was originally envisaged that this model would serve as a torpedo-bomber with external racks for two torpedoes. Accordingly, the pre-

(*Left*) *He 111J-1 bombers in service with Kü.Fl.Gr.806. A total of 90 total He 111J-1s was delivered to the Luftwaffe in the summer of 1938*

(*Above*) *The He* 111 *V18, a converted He 111D-0 to test bombing equipment, and* (*right*) *the He 111 V17 used as engine test-bed*

production **He 111J-0** aircraft featured no provision for internal bomb-bays, but a change in *Luftwaffe* policy resulted in the abandonment of plans to introduce the He 111J into service as a torpedo-bomber, and the reinstatement of the internal bomb-bays. Therefore, the 90 DB 600CG-powered **He 111J-1s** delivered to the *Luftwaffe* during the summer months of 1938 were identical in every respect to the He 111F-4s that were being delivered simultaneously, apart from the engines installed.

According to the OKL strength returns of September 19, 1938, nearly a half of the *Luftwaffe*'s first-line bomber strength of 1,235 twin-engined aircraft comprised He 111s, these totalling 570 machines. This total was made up of 272 He 111Bs, 171 He 111Es, 39 He 111Fs and 88 He 111Js, but by this time yet a further development in the prolific He 111

family had begun its journey down the assembly lines, the He 111P.

HEINKEL HE 111P

During 1937, a series of studies were initiated by the Heinkel team with a view to improving visibility for the crew and, simultaneously, the aerodynamic shape of the fuselage nose, and an He 111B-0 airframe was fitted with a new nose section and flown in January 1938 as the **He 111 V8** (D-AQUO). The shortened and broadened oval nose section of the V8 was a noteworthy departure from previous models. Whereas the pilot's windscreen had previously broken the upper fuselage contour in the conventional manner, this was now contained entirely within the contour of the fuselage, resulting in lines unbroken by any projection. The pilot was seated in the port side of the nose which was fully glazed, and this, the glazed roof and side windows provided the necessary vision.

The instrument panel was attached to the roof, and in order to provide the pilot with the

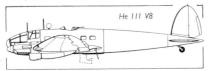

He III V8

maximum possible view, the universal mounting for the nose gun was offset to starboard, resulting in the peculiar asymmetric effect that was to characterise all He 111s manufactured from late 1938. For landing in poor visibility, the pilot could elevate his seat so that his head projected through a sliding panel, in which position it was protected from the slipstream by a small retractable windscreen. The new nose section offered the crew magnificent visibility, although when the sun was behind the aircraft the curved transparent panels tended to emulate mirrors, seriously inconveniencing the pilot.

With some rearrangement of the glazed panels, this nose reappeared in the early summer of 1938 on the **He 111 V7** which, two years earlier, had been the first aircraft to test the new, straight-tapered wing, and was now the production prototype for the He 111P series bomber. Apart from the new nose and straight-tapered wing, the He 111 V7 now

(*Left and below*) *The He 111 V8, a B-0 airframe used as a test-bed for the revised nose subsequently adopted for the P- and H-series*

(Above and right) An early production He 111P-1 (Werk-Nr. 2616), deliveries of which began during the early spring of 1939

featured a permanent, well-faired ventral gun position in which the gunner lay prone. This cupola, which supplanted the earlier retractable "dustbin", offered a 90° cone of fire for the protection of the underside and tail of the aircraft. One final refinement was a glazed hood for the dorsal gunner.

The He 111 V7 was powered by two Daimler-Benz DB 601Aa engines each rated at 1,150 h.p. for take-off and 1,020 h.p. at 14,765 ft., as was also the pre-production **He 111P-0** which followed the last He 111J from the Marienehe assembly line in the autumn of 1938. From the outset, the extensively revised bomber had been planned to take either Daimler-Benz or Junkers Jumo engines with equal facility owing to the immense demands being made on the former by the fighter production programme and the uncertainty of supplies in consequence, and a parallel development to the He 111P was the Jumo 211-engined He 111H. However, during the winter of 1938–39, supplies of DB 601 engines were not critical, and the RLM therefore gave priority to production of the He 111P, Heinkel's Marienehe and Dornier's Wismar factories being joined in the programme by one of the Arado plants at Warnemünde.

Deliveries of the initial production model, the **He 111P-1**, to the *Kampfgeschwader* began during the early spring of 1939, initially supplanting the now obsolescent He 111Bs. Possessing a maximum speed of 249 m.p.h. at 16,400 ft, and cruising at 230 m.p.h. at the same altitude without bomb load, these figures being reduced to 202 m.p.h. and 190 m.p.h. with maximum bomb load, the He 111P-1 carried a 4,410-lb. bomb load. Bombs were originally to have been housed by a bay of new design into which they were loaded horizontally, but as this change dictated extensive structural alterations, the earlier arrangement of individual vertical cells, four on each side of a gangway, was retained, the largest bomb that could be accommodated by these cells being a 551-pounder.

The most surprising feature of the He 111P-1 was perhaps the fact that it revealed no attempt to increase defensive armament which remained three 7.9-mm. MG 15 machine guns;

one mounted on an Ikaria spherical mounting in the glazed nose, one firing laterally or aft from the shielded dorsal position over the wing, and the other firing aft from the ventral gondola. The crew comprised the pilot on the port side, with the navigator/bombardier, who also operated the nose gun, seated on a tip-up seat to starboard, and the radio-operator, who also operated the dorsal gun, and the ventral gunner aft of the bomb-bays. The DB 601A-1 engines, which were each rated at 1,100 h.p. for take-off, drove three-blade variable-pitch VDM metal airscrews, and were fed from four self-sealing fuel tanks—two 155 Imp. gal. tanks inboard of the engine nacelles and two 226 Imp. gal. tanks outboard of the nacelles.

The structure of the He 111P-1 followed that of earlier bombers in the series in comprising a two-spar stressed-skin wing built in three sections, with the rectangular centre section built integral with the fuselage, an oval-section metal fuselage comprising three main bulkheads, a number of secondary frames interconnected by longerons and U-section stringers, and smooth metal skinning, and all-metal tail surfaces. Hydraulically-operated slotted flaps were carried by the

(Left) He 111P-1 bombers awaiting delivery to the Luftwaffe in the spring of 1939

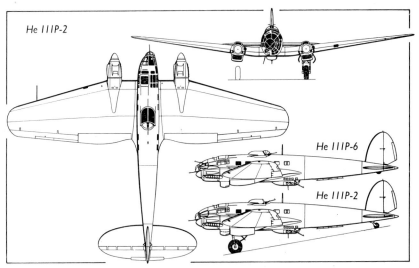

He 111P-2

He 111P-6

He 111P-2

The unique asymmetric nose of the He 111P-1 is clearly illustrated by the photograph (right)

inner sections of the wings, the outboard ailerons drooping automatically when the flaps were lowered, and the hydraulically-actuated main undercarriage members each comprised twin oleo legs with aft-sloping hinged members which raised the wheels aft into the tails of the engine nacelles.

In May 1939, the He 111P-1 was supplanted in production by the **He 111P-2** which differed solely in having the FuG III radio replaced by FuG 10, and in the same month

(*Above and left*) *He 111P-6 bombers of Kamfgeschwader 55 operational over the British Isles during the autumn and early winter of 1940*

1939, the *Kampfgeschwader* possessed 349 He 111P bombers of which 295 were serviceable. There were also 400 (358 serviceable) He 111H, 38 (32 serviceable) He 111E and 21 (20 serviceable) He 111J bombers on strength. The 111P was, like its companion the He 111H, an extremely efficient bomber with a good performance and excellent handling characteristics, but it possessed one major shortcoming—ineffective defensive armament. Possessing none of the power-operated turrets which characterized British medium bombers, the He 111's defensive armament had remained unaltered from the very first prototype, deliveries of the Jumo-engined He 111H-1 were initiated by the Oranienburg factory, the Junkers plant at Dessau and the new ATG plant at Leipzig also commencing deliveries of this version during the weeks that followed, production soon outstripping that of the DB 601-powered He 111P.

When hostilities began on September 1,

and was soon to be found woefully inadequate. Combat attrition over Poland, where fighter opposition was relatively weak and confined solely to obsolete PZL P.11c monoplanes, was markedly higher than had been anticipated by the High Command which had been deluded by the success of the He 111 over Spain, and efforts were immediately made to rectify the situation.

The He 111P-2 was supplanted in production by the **He 111P-4** (the **P-3** being a dual control trainer modification of early P-0 and P-1 airframes) which, while possessing a similar airframe and equipment to the P-2, introduced some armour protection for the pilot and for the dorsal and ventral gunner and heavier defensive armament. An additional forward-firing 7.9-mm. MG 15 was added to the nose armament, two further MG 15s were mounted to fire through side windows over the wing trailing edge to provide additional protection from beam attacks, a fifth member being added to the crew complement to operate these beam guns, and on some aircraft a single remotely-operated 7.9-mm MG 17 machine gun was fixed in the tail cone to discourage attacks from directly aft. Other changes introduced by the He 111P-4 included the blanking-off of the port bomb-bay which was occupied by a 183.5 Imp. gal. fuel tank and a 26 Imp. gal. oil tank, and the provision of two PVC 1006 external bomb racks beneath the blanked-off port bay. Provision was made for an additional pair of racks to be fitted beneath the starboard bay if required.

Production of the P-series bombers was finally phased out early in 1940 with the **He 111P-6** which introduced 1,175 h.p. DB 601N engines and otherwise differed from the P-4 only in reverting to the internal bomb-stowage arrangement of the P-2 and in having an improved dorsal gun position which could be completely enclosed. A number of these bombers were later to be adapted as tugs for cargo gliders under the designation **He 111P-6/R2**, and in 1942, a small number of

---

HEINKEL HE 111P-4 SPECIFICATION

Type: *Five-seat Medium Bomber.* **Power Plants:** *Two Daimler-Benz DB 601A-1 12-cylinder liquid-cooled engines each rated at 1,100 h.p. for take-off and 1,015 h.p. at 14,765 ft.* **Armament:** *(Defensive) One 7.9-mm. MG 15 machine gun on Ikaria flexible spherical mounting and one fixed forward-firing 7.9-mm. MG 15 in extreme nose, one 7.9-mm. MG 15 firing from each of two beam windows, one 7.9-mm. MG 15 on flexible mounting in dorsal position and ventral gondola and (optional) one fixed aft-firing 7.9-mm. MG 17 machine gun in tail cone. (Offensive) Four 551-lb. SC 250 bombs stowed vertically internally, and one or two 1,102-lb. SC 500 bombs externally.* **Performance:** *(Figures in parentheses relate to aircraft in maximum loaded condition.) Maximum speed, 225 (176) m.p.h. at sea level, 242 (190) m.p.h. at 6,560 ft., 247 (200) m.p.h. at 16,400 ft.; cruising speed at 85% power, 194 (168) m.p.h. at sea level, 212 (180) m.p.h. at 6,560 ft., 232 (193) m.p.h. at 16,400 ft.; maximum range, 1,224 mls. at 9,840 ft., with overload fuel, 1,490 mls.; time to 3,280 ft. at 29,762 lb., 7 min., to 6,560 ft., 14.2 min., to 14,765 ft., 31.3 min.; service ceiling (at 23,590 lb.), 26,250 ft., (at 29,762 lb.), 14,765 ft.* **Weights:** *Empty, 14,936 lb.; empty equipped, 17,670 lb.; maximum loaded, 29,762 lb.* **Dimensions:** *Span, 74 ft. 1¾ in.; length, 53 ft. 9½ in.; height, 13 ft. 1½ in.; wing area, 942.917 sq. ft.*

(Above and left) The He 111 V19, the prototype of the H-series bomber and first flown in January 1939

former *Luftwaffe* He 111P-6 bombers were transferred to the Hungarian Air Force to equip a night bomber squadron which operated continuously against Soviet targets until 1944.

The principal reason for the relatively limited production of the P-series by comparison with the H-series was the simple fact that whereas Daimler-Benz was still experiencing difficulties in keeping pace with the demands for its engines, Junkers had suffered no such difficulties, offering a ready supply of power plants. Furthermore, standardisation on one engine type, providing that the chosen power plant was readily available, offered obvious advantages.

HEINKEL HE 111H

Although production of the DB 601-powered He 111P and Jumo 211-powered He 111H was planned simultaneously, production deliveries of the latter to the *Luftwaffe* did not, in fact, commence until May 1939, the prototype for this model, the **He 111 V19** (D-AUKY) having flown for the first time in the previous January. Apart from their Jumo 211A-1 engines which were rated at 1,010 h.p. for take-off and 960 h.p. at 4,920 ft., the pre-production **He 111H-0** and initial production **He 111H-1** were identical to the He 111P-2, and a measure of the effort placed behind the H-series production programme may be gained from the fact that almost half the 808

He 111 bombers on the *Luftwaffe*'s first-line strength when the war began were of this version, some 400 examples having been delivered by the Heinkel company and its licensees within four months!

When World War II began, the He 111H assembly lines were in process of switching from the H-1 to the **H-2**, which, initially, differed from the first production model solely in having Jumo 211A-3 engines rated at 1,100 h.p. for take-off, but by October similar armament changes to those made on the He 111P-4 were being introduced on the He 111H-2 production line, basic defensive armament being increased from three to six 7.9-mm. MG 15s. In November 1939, yet another sub-type, the **He 111H-3**, made its début, this being intended both for normal bombing and anti-shipping operations, its only concession to the latter role being the introduction of a single forward-firing 20-mm. MG FF cannon in the ventral gondola. The effectiveness of this weapon was somewhat limited, however, by the small traverse possible and its relatively low rate of fire (540 r.p.m.). Embodying the heavier defensive armament of the He 111H-2, its normal crew complement was five members, but on occasions for anti-shipping strikes a sixth crew member could be carried. Power was provided by two Jumo 211D-1s rated at 1,200 h.p. for take-off, and the maximum bomb load of 4,410 lb. was carried internally, provision being made in the port bomb-bay for the installation of similar auxiliary fuel and oil tanks to those of the He 111P-4.

In the autumn of 1940, when a *Luftwaffe* mission took on the task of reorganising the Rumanian Air Force, a number of He 111H-3 bombers were supplied to the Rumanian government to supplement the S.M.79B medium bombers purchased from Italy, and on June 22, 1941, when German and Rumanian

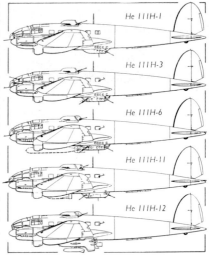

forces attacked the Soviet Union, the He 111H-3 equipped the three nine-aircraft squadrons (Nos. 78, 79 and 80) of No. 5 Group of the Rumanian Air Force's 1st Bomber Regiment. In 1940, preparations for the licence manufacture of the He 111H-3 had been initiated by the Fabrica de Avione S.E.T. at Bucharest, this concern commencing deliveries of licence-built aircraft to the Rumanian Air Force in 1942.

Production of the He 111H-3 continued throughout 1940, and early in 1941 the **He 111H-4** appeared, this being manufactured in parallel with the earlier model. The He 111H-4 was initially powered by similar Jumo 211D-1s

(Above) A pre-production He 111H-0 bomber photographed during pre-service trials in the late spring of 1939

to those of the H-3, but late production examples received the uprated Jumo 211F-1 which, having a strengthened crankshaft, a fully shrouded DVL supercharger impeller and other changes, offered 1,400 h.p. for take-off and 1,200 h.p. at 16,500 ft. Only the starboard bomb-bay was retained, and a heavy metal strengthening plate was added beneath the port side and to this were attached two PVC carriers for two 2,205-lb. bombs or one 3,968-lb. bomb, such loads being carried on short-range sorties.

The **He 111H-5** employed a similar basic airframe to that of the H-4, and like the earlier production examples of that variant, was powered by the Jumo 211D-1, but provision was made for auxiliary tanks in both port and starboard bomb-bays, and all offensive loads were normally carried externally on two PVC racks, the maximum overload weight of this variant rising to 30,982 lb., and maximum external load being 5,510 lb.

Both the H-4 and H-5 variants were progressively modified in the light of operational experience, these changes being incorporated both on the assembly lines and at forward maintenance units and modification centres,

but neither was produced in really large numbers, as all the progressive changes introduced on these sub-types were embodied in the He 111H-6 which succeeded the He 111H-3 as the next "standard" production version from late 1941.

Exhaustive trials had earlier been undertaken with all existing German bombers at the Grossenbrode bombing school in order to determine which was most suitable for adaptation for the torpedo-bombing role, and these and subsequent tests at Grosseto, on the West coast of Italy, had revealed the suitability of the He 111H. Accordingly, the He 111H-6 included among its various possible external offensive loads a pair of 1,686-lb. LT F5b torpedoes beneath the fuselage on PVC racks. Powered by similar Jumo 211F-1 engines to those of the late production H-4, the He 111H-6 possessed the augmented defensive armament first employed by the H-2 plus the forward-firing 20-mm. MG FF cannon introduced by the H-3. Some examples were fitted with the remotely-controlled 7.9-mm. MG 17 machine gun in the tail cone, and in place of this, others were experimentally fitted with a grenade launching tube from which grenades were ejected hopefully—but with little assurance of success—in the path of pursuing fighters.

The He 111H-6 rapidly became the most widely-used version of the Heinkel bomber, and was soon deployed on all the fronts on which the *Luftwaffe* was engaged. Popular with its crews and possessing pleasant handling qualities even at maximum weights, with good control characteristics and excellent stability and manoeuvrability, it was a supremely versatile warplane. It had been planned to commence phasing out production of the He 111H-6 during the early months of 1942 as it was anticipated that production of the He 177A heavy bomber and the Ju 288 medium bomber would have attained a sufficiently advanced stage to permit service introduction. The failure of both of these types, however, necessitated the expedient of once more stepping up the output of the He 111H, despite its fast approaching obsolescence. As the factories were already tooled-up for this type, it was relatively economical to manufacture in both man hours and materials, and it was easily maintained in the field. It could be used satisfactorily on the Russian front for tactical bombing because of the less formidable nature of the Soviet defences, although it lacked the range required for the strategic bombing of Russian industry.

Apart from conventional bombs, mines and torpedoes, it was hoped that the He 111H-6 would prove amenable to carrying the more advanced air-launched weapons that were under development, such as the *Fritz X* radio-guided bomb intended primarily for attacking armoured vehicles, the Blohm und Voss BV 246 *Hagelkorn* glider bomb, and the L 10 *Friedensengel* device intended to afford standard torpedoes gliding properties. In the spring of 1942, several He 111H-6s equipped with FuG 203 *Kehl* guidance transmitters were used for trials with the FX 1400 *Fritz X* at Foggia, southern Italy, but although some successes were achieved, the Heinkel did not prove entirely suitable as a carrier for this weapon which, in consequence, it was never equipped with for operational sorties. Other

(*Below*) *The rear-firing 7.9-mm. MG 17 gun installation in an He 111H-6 (Werk-Nr. 7064)*

He 111H-6s fitted with FuG 103 electric altimeters were employed for dropping tests with the BV 246 *Hagelkorn* (Hailstone) glider bomb, and trials were conducted with the *Friedensengel* (Angel of Peace) auxiliary lifting and stabilizing surfaces for torpedoes, but as with the *Fritz X*, the He 111H's role was confined to the test programmes conducted with these weapons and devices.

By this time, a profusion of minor equipment changes were taking place, both on the assembly lines and at modification centres, the **He 111H-7** and **H-9** indicating equipment changes in standard H-6 airframes, while the **He 111H-8** was a modification of earlier H-3 and H-5 airframes. The balloon barrages that protected many British industrial areas had proved troublesome to *Kampfgeschwader* endeavouring to make low-level pinpoint attacks, and a scheme was evolved whereby specially-adapted aircraft equipped with balloon-cable cutters would be sent against the target in advance of the main force whose path would thus be cleared of the balloon hazard. The result was the He 111H-8 equipped with combined balloon-cable fender and cutter gear taking the form of an immense

He 111H-2s (T5-BU left and T5-AU below) of the Aufklärungsgruppe Ob.d.L. at Oranienburg in 1940

(*Above*) *An He* 111*H-2 of Stab/KG* 53 *with additional nose and ventral MG* 15*s, and* (*right*) *an He* 111*H-2 of KG* 26 *with additional ventral MG* 15

ramework extending from a point some little istance ahead of the fuselage nose to both ingtips. This device weighed some 550 lb., nd it was necessary to provide an equivalent veight in ballast in the tail. This strictly mited the offensive load that the He 111H-8 as capable of carrying, and performance uffered markedly from the increased drag. hus, after relatively few operations over the ritish Isles, the survivors of the 30 aircraft onverted to this configuration were relegated the role of glider tugs under the designation e 111H-8/R2.

The next sub-type to be manufactured in me numbers was the **He 111H-10** which, enerally similar to the H-6 with the same rrangement of external bomb racks, had the ositions of the forward-firing MG 15 machine un and MG FF cannon transposed (the rmer being in the ventral gondola and the tter in the extreme nose), some increase in rmour protection for the crew, and the so- lled *Kuto-Nase*—built-in balloon-cable cut- rs on the wing leading edge. It was powered

by two Jumo 211F-2 engines as was also the He 111H-11 which supplanted the H-10 in production. While basically similar to its predecessor, the **He 111H-11** embodied yet further improvements in crew protection and defensive armament. For the first time the dorsal gun position was fully enclosed, pro- tective screens of armour-glass being provided and the standard 7.9-mm. MG 15 machine gun mounted in this position giving place to a 13-mm. MG 131. Aft defence was augmented by replacing the single MG 15 in the rear of the ventral gondola by a pair of 7.9-mm. MG 81 machine guns. A number of armour plates

(Above) An He 111H-4 with external PVC carriers on port side, and (left) an He 111H-5 (Werk-Nr. 3107) at Marienehe

were fitted to protect vulnerable areas, and these could be jettisoned in an emergency, and a special bomb-carrier plate beneath the fuselage provided racks for five 551-lb. bombs. Defensive armament was increased still further by forward maintenance units which replaced the beam-firing MG 15 machine gun on each side by two MG 81Z (twin MG 81s) installa-

tions to result in the **He 111H-11/R1**. Yet another derivative was the **He 111H-11/R2** with couplings to adapt it for glider-towing.

Although various of the more "exotic" weapons being developed in Germany had been tested on the He 111H, the first variant built specifically for launching one of these weapons was the **He 111H-12**. Lacking the ventral gondola featured by all previous He 111H series aircraft and carrying a crew of four, the He 111H-12 appeared early in 1943 and was intended to act as the carrier for two Henschel Hs 293A missiles. The FuG 203 *Kehl 111* transmitter which sent the control impulses to the FuG 230b *Strassburg* receiver mounted in the tail of the Hs 293A was installed in the dorsal gun position, while the actual missile controls were situated in the starboard side of the nose. The He 111H-12 launched the

Hs 293A missiles individually at a speed of about 210 m.p.h., taking up a position to port of the missile and then throttling back to about 160 m.p.h.

Relatively few He 111H-12s were produced and these were never used operationally. Earlier, an He 111H-6 had been used as a carrier aircraft in trials with the Hs 293G which was an attempt to add some of the advantages of the *Fritz X* to the Henschel missile, having a final "on target" glide angle of 60–80 deg. One of the first test drops took place on March 3, 1942, but only 10 examples of the Hs 293G were produced, this variant of the Henschel missile being abandoned in favour of the *Fritz X*. Two He 111H-12s were later employed in the test programme for the television-guided Hs 293D at Peenemünde-West from early October 1944.

The **He 111H-14** was a derivative of the H-10 intended for the pathfinder role and fitted with special radio equipment, including FuG *Samos* with Peil-GV (D/F installation) and APZ 5, plus FuG 351 *Korfu*. An initial batch of 30 aircraft of this type was built,

these mostly being used in 1944 by the *Sonderkommando* Rastedter of KG 40 operating from Bordeaux-Mérignac, and a further 20 had their special radio equipment removed before delivery, and fitted with glider-towing couplings were delivered to the Eastern Front as **He 111H-14/R2s**.

The **He 111H-16** may be considered the third "standard" production version of the H-series bomber, the first and second "standard" models being the H-3 and H-6 respectively, nearly all intervening sub-types being intended for special duties and carrying specialized equipment. The He 111H-16 actually preceded in production several of what, from their sub-type numbers, were ostensibly earlier models, and was a progressive development of the He 111H-6 with Jumo 211F-2 engines and embodying as standard all

(Right) An He 111H-6 with two practice torpedoes

123

the improvements that had been incorporated piecemeal in various versions in the light of operational experience. Defensive armament and armour followed the pattern set by the He 111H-11, and various alternative bomb arrangements were possible, the normal internal bomb-bays being retained or, when used to house auxiliary fuel tanks, ETC 2000 racks being fitted beneath the fuselage. The He 111H-16 could also take various *Rüstsätze*, or "standard equipment sets", and thus the **He 111H-16/R1** had an electrically-operated dorsal turret containing one 13-mm. MG 131

machine gun in place of the normal dorsal position; the **He 111H-16/R2** had a boom-type glider-towing coupling, and the **He 111H 16/R3** had additional armour protection and with reduced bomb load, served in the path finder role.

The **He 111H-18** was intended specifically for nocturnal operations basically similar to the He 111H-16/R3 but with similar radio equipment to that installed in the H-14 and like the earlier model, served with the *Sonder kommando* Rastedter of KG 40. All H 111H-18s were fitted with special flame damper exhausts.

Although the He 111H served mainly in th bombing role, it had been extensively used fo transport tasks on the Eastern Front sinc KG 4 had used its aircraft to drop supplies t *Wehrmacht* units caught in the Kholm pocke in the spring of 1942. Later in the year, tw special transport *Gruppen*, K.Gr.z.b.V.5 an 20, had been formed on obsolete models of th

(Left and below) He 111H-8 with combined balloon-cable fender and cutter gear of the type illustrated on the left on the opposite page

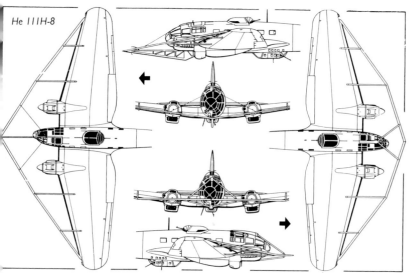

He 111H-8

He 111, and as the situation deteriorated, more and more He 111s were relegated from bombing to transport tasks. Thus, the next H-series model, the **He 111H-20**, was built from the outset for a variety of roles, including those of transport and glider-tug. With a similar basic airframe to that of the H-16, the He 111H-20 paratroop transport with crew of three and accommodation for 16 paratroops, a special central jump hatch and provision for two ,764-lb. supply containers on external racks; **I-20/R2** freighter and glider tug with crew of ive and electrically-operated dorsal turret

housing a single 13-mm. MG 131; **H-20/R3** night bomber with a single MG 131 in the nose, dorsal and ventral positions, plus twin 7.9-mm. MG 81s on two beam mountings and external racks for a 4,410-lb. bomb load, and the **H-20/R4** bomber intended for nocturnal harassing raids with an external load of 20 110-lb. bombs.

All H-series aircraft up to and including the He 111H-20 had been powered by Jumo 211 engines, but by early 1944 the Jumo 211 was being superseded in production by the more powerful Jumo 213, and the decision was taken to introduce this newer engine on the He 111H assembly line. The version of this power plant selected, the Jumo 213E-1 fitted with a three-speed two-stage supercharger and induction cooler, offered 1,750 h.p. for take-off and 1,320 h.p. at 32,000 ft., enabling maximum loaded weight to be raised from 35,275 lb., and maximum bomb load to 6,615 lb.

Some local structural strengthening accompanied the introduction of the new engines, but the basic airframe equipment and defensive armament were similar to those of the He 111H-20/R3, and the Jumo 213E-powered variant was allocated the designation **He 111H-21**. Owing to delays in the delivery of the new engines, the first 22 He 111H-21s were completed with Jumo 211F engines equipped with turbo-superchargers, but intended exclusively for the night bombing role, the new variant reached service status with its definitive engines in the late summer of 1944, proving

capable of a maximum speed without bomb load of 298 m.p.h.

Experiments conducted at Peenemünd during the winter of 1943–44 had confirmed the feasibility of launching the Fieseler Fi 10 (FZG 76) missile in the air from the He 111H and plans for continuing Operation *Rumpel kammer*—the bombardment of British target with Fi 103 missiles—by such means in the event of launching sites being lost were prepared well before the Allied assault on Europe commenced on June 6, 1944. By this time production of the He 111H was rapidly phasing out, but a number of He 111H-2 bombers already on the assembly line were modified to carry a single Fi 103 missile on simple rack under the port wing, between the engine and fuselage, under the designation He 111H-22. Simultaneously, a modification centre was set up at Oschatz to convert

number of He 111H-16 and H-20s as Fi 10 carriers. The planned method of operation was to release the missile by night from an altitude of 1,500 ft aiming it in the direction of a large city, i chances of falling in built-up area being considerable. After a short course in the technique of air-launching the

(Left) An He 111H modified to carry single FZG 76 missile under the port wing

03, III *Gruppe* of *Kampfgeschwader* 3 became operational with the He 111H missile carriers ate in July 1944, commencing operations against London and Southampton from bases n Holland late in that month.

The last few aircraft on the assembly line in he autumn of 1944 were completed as special aboteur transports under the designation He 111H-23. Carrying eight parachutists and eaturing a similar dropping hatch to that of he H-20/R1, the He 111H-23 was powered by wo Jumo 213A-1 engines each rated at 1,776 .p. for take-off and 1,600 h.p. at 18,000 ft. After delivery to the *Luftwaffe*, these aircraft vere converted as bombers by forward maintenance units.

With the He 111H-23, production of the Heinkel bomber finally terminated after nine ears (although licence production of the ie 111H-16 in Spain was to continue into the ifties), and although no exact figure for the otal quantity of He 111s of all types manuactured by the German aircraft industry is vailable, this is known to have exceeded ,300 machines of which 1,399 were produced 1 1939, 827 in 1940, 930 in 1941, 1,337 in 1942, ,408 in 1943 and 714 in 1944.

HEINKEL HE 111R

n 1943, consideration was given to the evelopment of a version of the Heinkel He 111 as an interim high-altitude bomber nder the designation He 111R. The initial roject, the He 111R-1, had two Jumo 211F ngines with annular radiators and turbouperchargers, but the estimated performance as considered insufficient, and in 1944 the He 111R-2 was proposed with Daimler-Benz B 603U engines fitted with either Hirth or KL 15 turbo-superchargers and having milar annular radiators to those proposed r the He 111R-1's Jumos. The DB 603U ffered 1,810 h.p. for take-off and 1,600 h.p. 42,000 ft., and estimated maximum speed

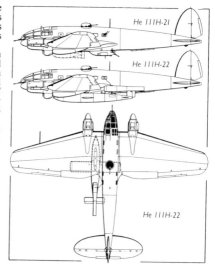

He 111H-21

He 111H-22

He 111H-22

of the He 111R-2 was 311 m.p.h., maximum loaded weight being 33,070 lb.

As a prototype for the He 111R, an He 111H-6 was equipped with DB 601U engines with TK 9 AC turbo-superchargers and annular radiators, and as the He 111 V32 this aircraft was tested early in 1944, but the development programme was abandoned shortly afterwards, and no examples of the He 111R were built.

OPERATIONAL CAREER

Immediately prior to the commencement of hostilities in Europe, the He 111-equipped *Kampfgeschwader* had virtually completed

HEINKEL HE 111H-16 SPECIFICATION

Type: *Five-seat Medium Bomber.* **Power Plants:** *Two Junkers Jumo 211F-2 12-cylinder liquid-cooled engines each rated at 1,350 h.p. for take-off and 1,060 h.p. at 17,390 ft.* **Armament:** *(Defensive) One 20-mm. MG FF cannon with 180 rounds in fuselage nose (additional 7.9-mm. MG 15 machine gun optional), one 13-mm. MG 131 machine gun with 1,000 rounds in dorsal position (electrically-operated dorsal turret in He 111H-16/R1), two 7.9-mm. MG 81 machine guns with 1,000 r.p.g. in rear of ventral gondola, and one 7.9-mm. MG 15 or MG 81 with 1,000 rounds or two 7.9-mm. MG 81 machine guns with 500 r.p.g. in each of two beam positions. (Offensive) Total of 32 110-lb. or eight 551-lb. bombs internally, or 16 110-lb. bombs internally and one 2,204-lb. bomb on external PVC rack, or one 4,410-lb. bomb and one 1,102-lb. bomb externally.* **Performance:** *Maximum speed without bombs and with half-fuel (figures in parentheses relate to aircraft in maximum loaded condition), 227 (217) m.p.h. at sea level, 248 (236) m.p.h. at 6,560 ft., 255 (242) m.p.h. at 13,120 ft., 270 (252) m.p.h. at 19,685 ft.; normal range with maximum bomb load, 1,212 mls. at 205 m.p.h. at sea level, 1,200 mls. at 230 m.p.h. at 6,560 ft., 1,280 mls. at 239 m.p.h. at 16,400 ft.; time to 6,560 ft. at maximum loaded weight, 8.5 min., to 13,120 ft., 23.5 min., to 19,685 ft., 42 min.; service ceiling (at maximum loaded weight), 21,980 ft., (without bomb load and with half fuel), 27,890 ft.* **Weights:** *Empty equipped, 19,136 lb.; maximum loaded, 30,865 lb.* **Dimensions:** *Span, 74 ft. 1¾ in.; length, 53 ft. 9½ in.; height, 13 ft. 1½ in.; wing area, 931.07 sq. ft.*

conversion to the P- and H-series of the bomber. The He 111 series were distributed as follows: (*Luftwaffe Lehr-Division*) *Stab*(K)/ LG 1, II/LG 1, III/LG 1 and 10.(K)/LG 2 with a total of 100 aircraft; (*Luftflotte* 1) *Stab*/KG 1, I/KG 1, I/KG 152, *Stab*/KG 4, and I, II and III/KG 4 with 184 aircraft; (*Luftwaffe* 2) *Stab*/KG 26, I and II/KG 26, *Stab*/KG 27, I, II and III/KG 27, and II/KG 28 with 204 aircraft, and (*Luftflotte* 3) *Stab*/KG 51, I and III/KG 51, *Stab*/KG 53, I, II and III/KG 53, *Stab*/KG 54, I/KG 54, *Stab*/KG 55, and I and II/KG 55 with a total of 301 aircraft. There were thus 21 *Gruppen* and one *Staffel* with a total of 789 aircraft.

The *Luftwaffe* Order of Battle against Poland on September 1, 1939 included the He 111s of *Kampfgeschwader* 1, 26 and 27 and *Lehrgeschwader* 1 under *Luftflotte* 1 in the North, and *Kampfgeschwader* 4 under *Luft-*

flotte 4 in the South. The He 111s of KG 1 attacked Polish fleet installations on the first morning of the war, their targets including seaplane bases, shore batteries and harbours along the Baltic coast. The *Gruppen* of this *Kampfgeschwader* later made deep penetration sorties East of the Vistula, and during the second week of the war were transferred South to the *Luftflotte* 4 area. *Kampfgeschwader* 26 participated only briefly in the Polish campaign before returning to North-West Germany for attacks on the British North Sea Fleet, but *Kampfgeschwader* 27, which took off from its peacetime bases on the afternoon of September 1st for the 470-mile flight to Warsaw to arrive over the Polish capital shortly after an attack delivered by LG 1 from East Prussia, was to be actively engaged throughout the campaign. Based in Silesia under *Luftflotte* 4, the I and III *Gruppen* of

Kampfgeschwader 4 began operations on the first day of the war with an attack on Cracow, while II/KG 4 bombed airfields at Lvov.

Although the results achieved by the He 111 during the Polish campaign were, in general, favourable, attrition was somewhat higher than had been anticipated, accounting for a large proportion of the 78 twin-engined bombers lost by the *Luftwaffe* during the campaign as a result of enemy fighters and anti-aircraft fire, and it was manifestly obvious that the He 111's defensive armament was inadequate.

By mid-September, the two *Gruppen* of KG 26 were based in North-West Germany under the 10.*Flieger-Division* which was being built up for the offensive against the Royal Navy and the British Isles across the North Sea. By the end of the month, the *Gruppen* were operating against British surface vessels at sea and, during October, carried out the first raids on British territory, attacking shipping in the Firth of Forth and Scapa Flow, and the first *Luftwaffe* aircraft brought down on British soil was an He 111P of *Stab*/KG 26 which force-landed near Dalkeith on October 28, 1939.

The He 111 formations allocated to

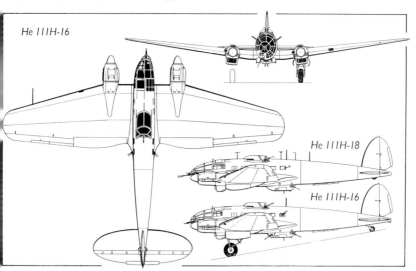

He 111H-16

He 111H-18

He 111H-16

Operation *Weserübung*, the occupation of Denmark and Norway, comprised *Kampfgeschwader* 4 based at Fasberg, Lüneberg, and Perleberg, *Kampfgeschwader* 26 based at Lübeck-Blankensee and Marx, and *Kampfgruppe* 100 based at Nordholz. Initially, these units were held in reserve or restricted to demonstrations of strength, and on the first morning of the invasion one *Gruppe* of KG 4 dropped leaflets over Copenhagen and another made a show of strength by flying over Kristiansand, Egersund, Stavanger and Bergen to coincide with the German seaborne and airborne landings. Simultaneously, the He 111s of III/KG 26 flew over Oslo Fjord where they were promptly attacked by Norwegian Gladiators. Subsequently, *Staffeln* of KG 4, KG 26 and KGr.100 bombed Oslo-Kjeller airfield, anti-aircraft emplacements on Holmenkollen, and coastal batteries on the islands in Oslo Fjord. On the following day, 41 He 111s from KG 26 in concert with 47 Ju 88As from KG 30 attacked the British Home Fleet off Bergen, damaging the cruisers, *Devonshire*, *Glasgow* and *Southampton*, and sinking the destroyer *Gurkha*. On April 10th, *Kampfgeschwader* 26 flew its He 111s into Norwegian bases from which they continued to support the ground operations of the *Wehrmacht*, remaining in Norway after the successful conclusion of *Weserübung* as part of *Luftflotte* 5, playing a part in the "Battle of Britain" by mounting attacks on North-East England across the North Sea.

For the onslaught on France and the Low Countries on May 10, 1940, *Luftflotten* 2 and 3 possessed a total of 1,120 twin-engined bombers of which approximately half were He 111s. At this time, two of the *Gruppen* of LG 1 had converted to the Ju 88A, the remaining *Gruppe* having 36 He 111s on strength. Both KG 4 and KG 51 were in process of converting to the Ju 88A, the former still possessing two *Gruppen* with a total of 80 He 111s on strength and the latter having one *Gruppe* with 42 He 111s. The *Kampfgeschwader* still completely He 111 equipped were KG 1 with 98 aircraft, KG 26 (based in Norway) with 99 aircraft, KG 27 with 106 aircraft, KG 53 with 112 aircraft, KG 54 with 110 aircraft, and KG 55 with 108 aircraft. In addition, *Kampfgruppe* 100 had 27 He 111s on strength for the pathfinder role, *Kampfgruppe* 126 possessed 32 He 111s for minelaying, and the *Fernaufklärungsgruppen* 120, 121 and 122 employed He 111s in conjunction with Do 17s and Ju 88s for reconnaissance.

By August 13, 1940, *Adlertag*, only four *Kampfgeschwader* were still completely equipped with He 111s, these being KG 26 which was still based in Norway, and KG 27 now based on Tours, KG 53 at Lille and KG 55 at Chartres. *Kampfgeschwader* 1's III *Gruppe* had converted to Ju 88As, KG 51 had completed conversion to the Ju 88A, and KG 54's I and II *Gruppen* had converted to the Ju 88A while III *Gruppe* was in process of conversion. After the initial strikes across the Straits of Dover, the first sorties in force by He 111s took place on August 15th when 63 aircraft of I and III/KG 26 flew from Stavanger with the intention of attacking the R.A.F. bases at Dishforth and Linton-upon-Ouse, and escorted by the Bf 100C fighters of I/ZG 76. Owing to a navigational error none found its target, and intercepted by R.A.F. fighters, the two *Gruppen* of KG 26 suffered heavy casualties.

Daylight attacks by the He 111 formations continued despite heavy attrition, but such were the casualties being suffered that by mid-September a change of tactics became imperative, and from the 16th of that month the He 111 was largely confined to nocturnal sorties. On the night of November 14th, two *Staffeln* of *Kampfgruppe* 100 took-off from

Vannes to employ beam approach methods for the first time. K.Gr.100's He 111H-3's were equipped with the so-called X-*Geräten*, receiving high-frequency signals from a *Knickebein* transmitter on the French coast which directed a radio beam directly at the target—in this case Coventry. In the meantime, the remaining two He 111-equipped *Gruppen* of *Kampfgeschwader* 4 were engaged in mining harbour approaches and the routes taken by coastal convoys.

The assault on Britain finally petered out in October 1940. The He 111 had finally been tested under conditions in which effective defences were encountered and it had been found vulnerable. Its defensive armament was

too meagre, its range was too limited and its bomb load was inadequate. The bulk of the He 111-equipped units remained in the West until May 1941, undertaking desultory night attacks. Exceptions were II/KG 26 which was transferred in January 1941 from Norway to Sicily for anti-shipping operations in the Mediterranean, and II/KG 4 which, in April, was transferred from channel mining operations to Rumania from where it carried out mining sorties against the Suez Canal. Later, a detachment was sent from this *Gruppe* to

(*Right*) *An He* 111H-11 *of KG 55 participating in Operation Steinbock against London early in* 1944, *and* (*below*) *an He* 111E-8/R2 *glider tug*

Iraq where it operated under temporary Iraqi colours until the lack of spares and replacements forced the return of the parent unit for participation in the assault on the Soviet Union.

At the end of May 1941, the bulk of the He 111s began their move eastward in the build-up for the attack on the Soviet Union on June 22nd, the participating He 111-equipped units, all of which had by this time re-equipped with H-series aircraft, being KG 27, KG 53, and KG 55, these *Kampfgeschwader* being joined a month later, on July 26th, by KG 4 whose III *Gruppe* had now reverted to the He 111H from the Ju 88A. By August 16, 1941, only 128 serviceable He 111Hs were operating with the four *Kampfgruppen* in Russia, plus seven aircraft with K.Gr.100. At this date there were also 19 He 111s with II/KG 26 in the Mediterranean, six He 111s of III/KG 40 under *Luftflotte* 3 in the West attached to the *Fliegerführer Atlantik*, and 30 He 111s were with the *Stab* and I and III/KG 26 in Norway. Thus, excluding aircraft serving in the reconnaissance, communications and training roles, and second-line aircraft, there were only 190 serviceable front-line He 111 bombers in *Luftwaffe* service at this time!

The most noteworthy employment of the He 111 came with the delivery of He 111H-6s suitable for torpedo attack to KG 26 in Norway. By the end of April 1942, I/KG 26 had become operational, followed by III/KG 26 in June, at the newly constructed airfields of Banak and Bardufoss in Norway for attacks on convoys sailing via the Arctic to Murmansk and Archangel. The first 11 PQ convoys over this route had been virtually unmolested, but in February 1942, PQ 13 had been attacked, and between May 25th and 30th PQ 16 was heavily attacked by the Ju 88s of KG 30 and the He 111H-6s of I/KG 26, seven out of 35 vessels being sunk. The most spectacular *Luftwaffe* attack on an Arctic convoy was that on the ill-fated PQ 17 in which I/KG 26's He 111H-6s again participated in concert with the Ju 88s of KG 30. In this action, which took place between July 5th and 10th, 23 vessels were lost out of a total of 36. Both I and III/KG 26 were involved in the attacks on PQ 18 between the 13th and 14th of September, and of the 13 vessels sunk, 10 were

(Below) An He 111H-16/R1, this version introducing an electrically-operated dorsal turret mounting a single 13-mm. MG 131 machine gun

(*Above and right*) *He 111H-3 bombers of the Rumanian Air Force manufactured by Fabrica de Avione S.E.T. at Bucharest*

the victims of torpedoes launched by the He 111H-6s.

Meanwhile, on the Eastern Front, the He 111 units were being increasingly relegated to transport and supply missions as the situation deteriorated, and by the end of 1942 the major proportion of the He 111s in Russia were undertaking transport tasks in support of the attempted relief of Stalingrad. On November 24, 1942, *Luftflotte* 4 had begun the attempted aerial relief of the Stalingrad pocket, but it was soon evident that the 11 *Gruppen* of Ju 52/3m transports available were inadequate for the task. Thus, on November 30th the He 111 joined the airlift for the first time. In addition to two specially-formed He 111 transport *Gruppen*, K.Gr.z.b.V.5 with a mixture of He 111P-2s, P-4s, H-2s, H-3s and H-6s, and K.Gr.z.b.V.20 with He 111Es, Fs, P-4s and H-3s, the *Stab* and I, II and III/KG 55, I/KG 100, and I, II and III/KG 27 with He 111H-6s, H-11s, H-14s and H-16s were all applied to the task of supplying the German 6th Army. The supreme effort made by the

He 111 units in supplying Stalingrad during the period between November 24, 1942 and January 31, 1943 is reflected by the fact that they lost no fewer than 165 aircraft, representing more than half the He 111s employed, and a blow from which the *Kampfgeschwader* were never to recover.

For the He 111 bombing became virtually a secondary task in 1943 as progressively stronger emphasis was placed on air-supply of retreating or beleaguered German forces, and during the course of the year more He 111 transport *Gruppen* were formed, and the type was introduced as a tug for Gotha Go 242

An He 111H-6 with 50-mm. anti-tank gun in so-called Dobbas transporter pack attached to external racks

gliders with *Luftlandegeschwader* 1. Although offensive bombing missions in strength by He 111s were no longer commonplace, an outstanding night attack was performed on June 22, 1944 by all four He 111 *Kampfgeschwader* (KG 4, 27, 53 and 55) against B-17 Fortresses at Poltava. The airfield was lit by flares dropped by KG 4, and during the attack some 43 B-17s and 15 P-51 Mustangs were destroyed.

The He 111 achieved some prominence once more in the summer of 1944 when He 111H-22s and converted He 111H-16s and H-20s of III/KG 3 began launching Fi 103 (FZG 76) missiles against Britain as a continuation of Operation *Rumpelkammer*. The missile-launching operations of III/KG 3 were begun from Venlo in Holland at the end of July, and the *Gruppe* had aimed some 300 Fi 103s at London and a further 90 at Southampton, as well as about 20 at Gloucester by the end of August. In September 1944, KG 53 was pulled back from the Eastern Front, its I *Gruppe* being disbanded, the crews being

transferred to II and III/KG 53 to bring them up to strength. In the meantime, III/KG 3 had been redesignated I/KG 53, and in November 1944 this *Gruppe* was joined on missile-launching sorties by II/KG 53 operating from airfields in the Oldenburg-Bremen area. In September KG 27 had been disbanded and its surviving aircraft, hurriedly adapted for missile-launching at Oschatz, were issued to III/KG 53 which was ready for operations by the beginning of December.

After a lull between September 5th and 15th while I/KG 53 transferred from Venlo to North-West Germany, Fi 103 launching operations were resumed on September 16th, airborne launchings being made on most nights up to the end of the month, a total of 177 missiles being despatched. This total increased to 282 in October and 316 in November, but the hazardous nature of the operations took heavy toll of KG 53, II *Gruppe*, for example, losing 12 aircraft in two operations as a result of Fi 103 missiles detonating just after their carrier aircraft had taken off. Launching operations finally terminated on January 14, 1945, and from first to last the launching units had lost 77 aircraft from all causes, and more than 1,200 missiles having been despatched against the British Isles.

On April 25, 1945, all remaining He 111s in *Luftwaffe* service had been relegated to the transport role with the exception of 27 aircraft on the strength of a certain *Gruppe* Uhl which, based at Rerik under *Luftflotte Reich*, specialised in nocturnal attacks on railway targets. The transport units comprised I/KG 4 with 25 He 111s at Königgrätz, II/KG 4 with 28 He 111s at Greifswald, III/KG 4 with 23 He 111s at Königgrätz, and Tr.Gr.30 with 16 He 111s at Neubiberg. In addition, 15 He 111 glider tugs were on the strength of *Schleppgruppe* 1 at Königgrätz.

HEINKEL HE 116B

In 1936, the German airline Deutsche Lufthansa (DLH) began to evince interest in the possibilities of direct mail services to the Far East. The route contemplated by DLH necessitated crossing the Pamir mountain range on the Afghanistan-Tadzhikistan border, dictating a service ceiling in excess of 25,000 feet, and on the premise that high-altitude engines in the 500 h.p. category would be available during the course of the next two years, the Ernst Heinkel Flugzeugwerke initiated the design of a four-engined long-range monoplane specifically to meet DLH's needs.

Progress with airframe construction was more rapid than that with the Hirth high-altitude engine which it was intended should provide the power, and the first prototype, the **He 116 V1**, was completed in the spring of 1937 with four Hirth HM 508C eight-cylinder inverted-vee air-cooled engines driving two-bladed VDM variable-pitch airscrews and each rated at 270 h.p. for take-off. The

(Right) The He 116 V8 (D-ADOG), and (below) one of the six He 116B-0 aircraft

Although resembling that of later He 111s, the nose of the He 116B-0 (left) lacked the asymmetry so characteristic of the nose of the bomber

second, similarly-powered aircraft, the **He 116 V2** (D-AJIE), was intended as the production prototype, and, in 1938, was de-

---

HEINKEL HE 116B-0 SPECIFICATION

Type: *Four-seat Long-Range Photographic-Reconnaissance Aircraft.* **Power Plants:** *Four Hirth HM 508H eight-cylinder inverted-vee air-cooled engines each rated at 240 h.p. for take-off.* **Performance:** *Maximum speed, 202 m.p.h. at 9,840 ft., 178 m.p.h. at sea level; maximum cruising speed, 186 m.p.h. at 9,840 ft., 162 m.p.h. at sea level; economical cruising speed (30 per cent power) 164 m.p.h. at 9,840 ft., 142 m.p.h. at sea level; range, 2,120 mls. at 9,840 ft., 1,980 mls. at sea level; climb to 3,280 ft., 4.2 min., to 13,120 ft., 17 min.; service ceiling (at maximum loaded weight), 21,325 ft.* **Weights:** *Empty, 8,862 lb.; loaded, 15,533 lb.* **Dimensions:** *Span, 72 ft. 2 in.; length, 46 ft. 11 in.; height, 10 ft. 10 in.; wing area, 677 sq. ft.*

---

livered to DLH for evaluation as the *Schlesien*, together with the **He 116A-02** alias **V4** (D-ATIO) *Hamburg*. Although the intended engines had still failed to materialize and, in the event, were to be abandoned, Heinkel had completed the four pre-production He 116A-0 aircraft (all of which were allocated *Versuchs* numbers) by the beginning of 1938, together with two additional prototypes, the **He 116 V7** and **V8**, modified for the long-range photographic role to the requirements of the *Reichsluftfahrtministerium* (RLM).

Two of the He 116A-0 aircraft had, in the meantime, been ordered by the Japanese, these being registered J-BAKD and J-EAKF and named *Nogi* and *Togo* respectively. The two aircraft left Tempelhof, Berlin, for Japan on April 23, 1938, reaching Tokyo six days later, completing the 9,532 miles in a total flying time of 54 hr. 17 min. These were subsequently operated by Manchurian Air Lines over the Tokyo-Hsingking route. One other A-series aircraft, the **He 111A-03** alias **V3** (D-ARFD), was modified in 1938 for distance record-breaking purposes. The wing span and area were increased to 82 ft. and 813.75 sq. ft. respectively, fuel tankage was substantially augmented, and HM 508H engines were installed, these operating at lower r.p.m. and featuring a slight reduction in supercharging to provide a maximum output of 240 h.p. for take-off. Designated **He 116R** and named *Rostock*, the aircraft was equipped with four take-off assistance rockets, but during the take-off for the initial attempt on the distance record one of the rockets tore loose and severely damaged the wing. After repairs, the He 116R took-off successfully on June 30

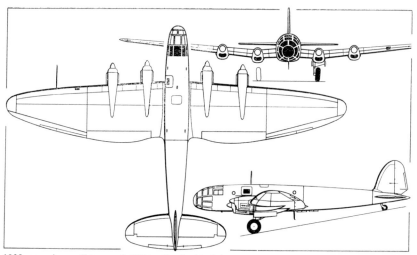

1938, covering a distance of 6,214 miles in 46 hr. 18 min. at an average speed of 134 m.p.h.

The He 116 V7 and V8 differed little structurally from their predecessors but featured a completely redesigned and extensively glazed nose section, and six additional aircraft were ordered by the RLM for specialized extended-endurance reconnaissance and photographic missions. Delivered to the *Luftwaffe* in 1938 as **He 116B-0**s, these aircraft were, like their predecessors, also allocated *Versuchs* numbers (V9 to V14), and the intention was to employ them for extreme-range surveillance missions. No provision was made for defensive armament as it was anticipated that they would operate far outside the range of any land-based fighters.

The He 116B featured a duralumin oval-section monocoque fuselage with watertight bulkheads, and a two-spar wooden wing with plywood skinning. Four crew members were carried, comprising pilot, co-pilot, radio-operator and navigator, and provision was made for the installation of various cameras. The He 116V7 and V8 and the six He 116Bs were issued to various *Luftdienstkommandos* immediately prior to the war, and proposals were made for their use for various reconnaissance tasks but they were destined never to fly beyond any frontline, continuing in *Luftdienst* service and performing photographic missions over Germany and German-occupied territory.

In the early 'thirties, the Heinkel He 70 created by Siegfried and Walter Günter was probably more responsible for re-establishing Germany among the leading aircraft-designing nations than any other single aircraft type. The Günter brothers possessed a remarkable feeling for the aesthetic in aircraft design, and the He 70 was, for its time, an outstanding example of aerodynamic refinement. Its duralumin monocoque fuselage was superbly contoured and every rivet was countersunk, its 630 h.p. BMW VI 6.0Z engine was closely cowled, and it established a pattern in wings of elliptical form that were to be considered almost a Heinkel trademark. What is more, when the prototype of this four-passenger commercial monoplane made its début on December 1, 1932, it could display a clean

pair of heels to any European fighter extant.

Dubbed the *Blitz* (Lightning), the He 70 gained considerable publicity for Deutsche Lufthansa (DLH) from June 15, 1934, when the airline introduced the type on its regular services, but somewhat less publicity attended the adoption of a military derivative by the fledgeling *Luftwaffe* for the attack bomber and high-speed reconnaissance tasks. The career of the He 70 in first-line *Luftwaffe* service was destined to be relatively brief, the type being relegated to the *Kurierstaffeln* long before the first shots of World War II were fired. However, although the He 70 was confined to more pacific tasks than bombing and reconnaissance when the *Luftwaffe* went to war, an export development of the basic design, the He 170 was to see action in Hungarian service.

The pre-production He 170A-01 which, flown early in 1937, differed from the V1 in having extended engine bearers to eradicate some c.g. problems

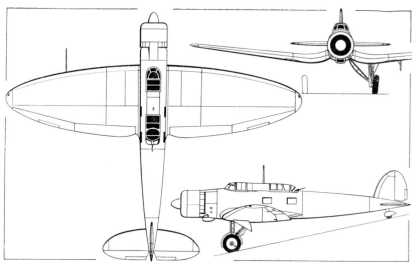

The Manfred Weiss Flugzeug und Motoren-fabrik at Budapest had acquired a manu-facturing licence for the Gnôme-Rhône 14K Mistral-Major 14-cylinder radial air-cooled engine in the mid 'thirties, and in 1936, the Hungarian government, in defiance of the Versailles Treaty, having sponsored the establishment of a clandestine air arm, began to evince interest in the possibility of installing the Gnôme-Rhône in the He 70 airframe. Heinkel accordingly made a test installation in an He 70F-3 airframe as the **He 170 V1** (D-OASA). Initially, the engine bearers of the radial engine were attached directly to the forward main frame in the fashion of the

BMW VI liquid-cooled inline engine that it replaced, but c.g. difficulties necessitated extending the forward fuselage, this modi-fication being introduced on the **He 170A-01** (D-OHEW) which, powered by a Manfred Weiss-built WM-K-14 driving a three-blade variable-pitch Hamilton Standard airscrew, was flown early in 1937.

The He 170A-01 was the first aircraft in a batch of 20 ordered by the Hungarian govern-ment and delivered late in 1937 to equip the Hungarian Air Force's 1st Independent Long-Range Reconnaissance Group which was formed with two squadrons, each of nine aircraft, at Mátyásföld, near Budapest.

Gebauer machine guns on a flexible mounting in the rear cockpit.

OPERATIONAL CAREER

At the end of 1938, the He 170A-equipped Group was transferred to Kecskemét from where it flew its first operational sorties in March 1939, when the Hungarian Army reoccupied Carpatho-Ruthenia. During the summer of 1940, the situation between Rumania and Hungary became extremely tense

Structurally, the He 170A was identical to the He 70F-3. The one-piece wing was built up of two spruce and plywood box spars, with closely-spaced wooden ribs and plywood skinning, and housed two 47 Imp. gal. fuel tanks and the main members of the hydraulically-retractable undercarriage. The fuselage was an oval duralumin monocoque and provided accommodation for three crew members—pilot, navigator/camera-operator, and radio-operator/gunner—and defensive armament was confined to a pair of 7.8-mm.

over the latter's demand for the return of Transylvania, and the He 170As flew many clandestine photographic sorties over the disputed territory at altitudes between 19,000 and 26,000 feet, successfully eluding Rumanian interceptors and continuing these operations until the return to Hungary of northern Transylvania in August 1940 eased tension between the two countries.

Early in November 1940, the Group was transferred to Budaörs, near Budapest, but low temperatures stopped all flying as the

He 170A proved unserviceable under such conditions. It was found that only a minimum of icing on the radio aerial resulted in this vibrating severely and eventually snapping off. In April 1941, with the commencement of the Balkan campaign, the He 170s were once more active, undertaking low-level reconnaissance and photographic missions for the Hungarian Army when it occupied the Bácska territory that had been ceded to Yugoslavia, and the He 170A's first sortie over Soviet territory took place on June 26, 1941. About a score of additional missions were flown by the He 170As from Budaörs, the aircraft landing to refuel at Ungvar after reconnoitring the Sambor, Gorodok, Lvov, Brody, Tarnopol, Chortkov, Dunayevtsy, Kements and Podolsk areas. During this period only one He 170A was shot down by Russian fighters, and another was lost in a forced landing after exhausting its fuel.

Despite low combat losses, the He 170A was anything but popular with its crews as it burned readily when hit, its defensive armament was considered totally inadequate and its field of fire poor, the field of vision offered was strictly limited and it was short on range. This last-mentioned short-coming finally prompted the Hungarian High Command to

withdraw the He 170A from first-line operational service after fewer than 30 missions had been flown.

(Right) The He 170A, although possessing extremely graceful lines, proved itself an unsatisfactory combat aircraft in Hungarian service. The He 170A-01 is illustrated

In view of the fact that the *Luftwaffe*'s first Chief-of-Staff, Lieut. General Wever, energetically and persistently championed the cause of the long-range heavy bomber, believing such to be a decisive factor in any future European conflict, it is perhaps surprising that the service possessed no warplanes in this category when hostilities in Europe began.

Wever had demanded bombers capable of carrying heavy loads to targets anywhere in the British Isles; aircraft possessing sufficient range to harass British shipping far out in the Atlantic. With Wever's death German heavy bomber development virtually stagnated until, in 1938, a belated reappraisal of his theories led the *Technische Amt* of the *Reichsluftfahrtministerium* to draft a specification for a new heavy bomber; a specification issued to one aircraft manufacturer only—the Ernst Heinkel Flugzeugwerke. In the course of time, this specification took material form in the shape of the He 177 *Greif* (Griffon) which was destined to provide the most dismal chapter in the wartime record of the German aircraft industry. Few aircraft that attained service status during World War II were less popular with their crews than this heavy bomber. Its shortcomings and teething troubles accompanied the bomber onto operations, and the result was a singularly inauspicious service career.

Fires in the air, aerodynamic troubles and structural failures were all to play prominent parts in the history of the He 177 *Greif*. It was to encounter difficulties from its birth, the causes of which were to be recognised too late, and when finally recognised they were subjected to insufficiently energetic attempts to eradicate them. Not that there was anything *basically* wrong with the design of the He 177, which probably embodied as much ingenuity as any German wartime aircraft, and had effective measures been taken to solve the problems that it presented at a sufficiently early stage in its career, the *Luftwaffe*'s

(Below) The He 177 V1 (Werk-Nr. 00 001) which was flown for the first time on November 19, 1939 by Dipl.Ing. Francke of the E-Stelle at Rechlin

(Above) The He 177 V2 which disintegrated in a shallow dive during an early phase of the bomber's flight test programme

Kampfgeschwader might have found themselves operating adequate quantities of a bomber with which they could sustain a major strategic bombing offensive.

The reasons for the He 177's prolonged gestatory period were, of course, many and varied, but major contributory factors were undoubtedly vacillation on the part of the RLM, conflicting military and political policies, and petty jealousies and commercial rivalry within the aircraft industry itself. When Ernst Heinkel submitted the He P.1041 proposal to the *Technische Amt* in the late spring of 1938, however, he envisaged that production status could be attained by the new bomber within two years with service deliveries commencing late in 1940 or early in 1941.

In 1938, Dipl.Ing. Heinrich Hertel had been Heinkel's Technical Director and Chief of Development for some four years, and the task of producing the P.1041 design study was entrusted to one of the most talented members of his team, Siegfried Günter. The RLM specification had called for an aircraft capable of carrying a bomb load of at least 2,000 lb. over a range of 4,160 miles. It had to possess a maximum speed of not less than 335 m.p.h., and it had to possess sufficient structural strength to enable it to undertake medium-angle diving attacks. The P.1041 proposal as drafted by Günter embodied many advanced and, in some respects, revolutionary features, such as coupled power plants (two engines paired in one nacelle and driving a common airscrew) with surface evaporation cooling. The estimated loaded weight of the bomber was 59,520 lb., and it was anticipated that the aircraft would be capable of attaining a maximum speed of 342 m.p.h. at 18,000 ft.—a speed appreciably higher than attained by most contemporary single-seat fighters.

Günter's project was accepted by the *Technische Amt* and allocated the official RLM type number He 177, but its creator was already having second thoughts concerning the wisdom of incorporating so many unproven features. However, the consensus of opinion was that any problems presented by the more radical aspects of the bomber could be overcome by the time the first prototype could be ready for flight testing, and detail design was initiated without any major departures from the original draft proposal.

One of the most radical features of the He 177 was its coupled power plants—two 12-cylinder liquid-cooled engines mounted side-by-side with a single gear casing connecting the two crankcases, the two crankshaft pinions driving a single airscrew shaft gear. The use of two power plants of very large output in a heavy bomber was undoubtedly sounder aerodynamically than that of four separate engines of smaller capacity, offering substantial drag reduction and a marked improvement in manoeuvrability. The coupled power plant principle also avoided the uncertainty and delay attendant upon the development of an entirely new engine offering comparable power, while production was simplified since the same basic units could serve both in orthodox single installations and for the coupled arrangement. In the He 177, the coupled power plant—the Daimler-Benz DB 606 which comprised two DB 601 engines mounted side-by-side and inclined so that the inner banks of cylinders were disposed almost vertically—was combined with a system of surface evaporation cooling to augment the orthodox radiators, but despite the immense amount of research undertaken by Heinkel into the problems of surface evaporation cooling, by the spring of 1939, Günter was forced to admit that his earlier forebodings had some substance, and the first major change to the original concept was made, the provision of orthodox radiators large enough to provide sufficient cooling without being supplemented by surface evaporation cooling.

The larger radiators naturally added to airframe drag, reducing both speed and range, and in order to maintain the latter figure to that originally specified, it was found necessary to make provision for additional fuel cells in the wings. These, in turn, necessitated some structural strengthening with attendant increases in weight and, thus, a further reduction in anticipated performance.

Another design innovation featured by the He 177 as originally conceived was the use of remotely-controlled defensive gun barbettes which offered substantially less drag than manned turrets. Work on remotely-controlled aircraft defensive systems had reached a relatively advanced stage in Germany in the late 'thirties, but progress in this field was insufficient to keep pace with the He 177, and the design had once more to be modified; this time to accommodate manned turrets with, of course, a further increment of drag.

An even more serious problem, however, was that posed by the insistence of the *Technische Amt* that the heavy bomber be capable of performing 60° diving attacks rather than the medium-angle dives called for by the

(*Left*) *The He 177 V4 landing during an early test. It later crashed into the sea near Ribnitz*

144

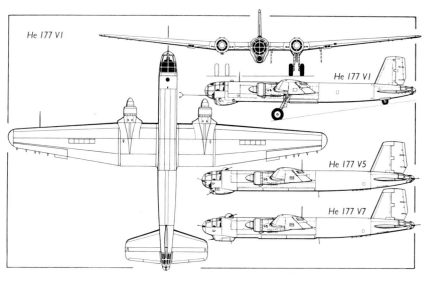

He 177 V1

He 177 V1

He 177 V5

He 177 V7

original specification. In order to withstand the tremendous stresses that would be imposed on an aircraft of the He 177's size during the pull-out from such a dive, further structural strengthening was dictated. By this time the anticipated gross weight of the bomber had increased so alarmingly that the provision of an undercarriage of sufficient strength began to pose a major problem. Neither the engine nacelles nor the wings, which were of low thickness/cord ratio, provided much stowage space for the main undercarriage members, and after several extremely complex arrangements had been considered, a rather novel system was adopted. Two massive single-wheel oleo legs were attached to the main spar at each engine nacelle, the outboard legs retracting upward and outward into shallow wing wells, the inboard legs swinging upward and inward into similar wells in the wing roots, all units being completely enclosed by flush-fitting doors.

The *Oberkommando der Luftwaffe* (OKL) was, meanwhile, evincing only luke-warm interest in the He 177. Major-General Hans Jeschonnek, who had succeeded Stumpff as Chief of Air Staff, was convinced that Germany should concentrate on production of the

shorter-range medium bomber which he believed would, if available to the *Luftwaffe* in sufficient numbers, deter Britain and France from aiding Poland. It was decided, therefore, to virtually abandon the heavy bomber and gamble on Britain staying out of any future conflict; a gamble which was to prove one of the greatest single mistakes made by the German High Command in planning its future strategy. The Admiralty was insistent that such an aircraft as the He 177 was necessary for co-operation with the U-boat fleet and for long-range offensive reconnaissance over the Atlantic, however, and it was decided to continue construction of the prototypes rather than abandon the entire programme.

By the summer of 1939, it was becoming increasingly obvious to the High Command that Britain and France *would* go to the aid of Poland in the event of that country being attacked, and the OKL began to evince a renewal of interest in the He 177, urging Heinkel to hasten prototype construction. Unfortunately, during the previous March, Dipl. Ing. Hertel had left Heinkel and this did not augur well for the future of the bomber.

PROTOTYPE DEVELOPMENT

Aerodynamically, the He 177 was a large, well-proportioned, mid-wing monoplane which, from the structural viewpoint, offered few novelties. Conventional metal stressed-skin construction was employed, and the wing was built up on a single main spar. On November 19, 1939, the first prototype, the **He 177 V1** (*Werk-Nr.00 001*), was flown for the first time with Dipl. Ing. Francke, chief of the Rechlin *Erprobungsstelle* E-2 flight test section, at the controls. This initial flight terminated abruptly after only 12 minutes as the engine temperatures began to rise alarmingly. Francke referred favourably to the take-off, general handling and landing characteristics of the prototype but complained of some vibration in the airscrew shafts, the inadequacy of the tail surfaces under certain conditions, and some flutter which accompanied any vigorous movement of the elevators.

The He 177 V1 had an empty equipped weight of 30,247 lb., and loaded weight was 52,734 lb. Overall dimensions included a span of 103 ft. 0¼ in., an overall length of 67 ft. 6¼ in., a height of 21 ft. 10½ in., and a wing area of 1,076.39 sq. ft. Maximum speed at 286 m.p.h., nearly 50 m.p.h. below that demanded by the original specification, was more than a little disappointing, as was also the maximum cruising speed of 255 m.p.h., and maximum range at 3,107 miles was some 25 per cent below that demanded. Although provision was made for a single 13-mm. MG 131 machine gun above and immediately aft of the flight deck, a similar gun in the ventral gondola and a third in the extreme tail, no armament was actually installed, and only the aft bomb-bay was fitted. This bomb-bay projected slightly below the lower fuselage contour as a result of an increase in bomb calibres during the construction of the prototype.

The second prototype, the **He 177 V2** (*Werk-Nr.*00 002), followed closely behind the He 177 V1, and was flown on its maiden flight by Francke, and in the meantime, the initial aircraft received several modifications suggested by initial trials, including a 20 per cent increase in tail surface area, subsequently being flown to the Rechlin *Erprobungsstelle*. These modifications were not applied to the He 177 V2 when another E-2 test pilot, Rickert, undertook the first diving trials. Serious control surface flutter developed immediately the pilot entered the dive and the machine disintegrated. After this incident, the tail surfaces of the third, fourth and fifth prototypes nearing completion at Rostock-

Marienehe were modified in a similar fashion to those of the He 177 V1.

The torsional vibration in the airscrew drive shafts which had manifested itself on the bomber's first flight was relatively simple of solution by comparison with the problem of engine overheating which was to result in a proclivity towards catching fire in mid-air and the uncomplimentary epithet of "*Luftwaffenfeuerzeug*" (Luftwaffe's Lighter). The **He 177 V3** (*Werk-Nr.*00 003), which bore the civil registration D-AGIG, was allocated the task of power plant development, for which purpose it was flown to Rechlin in mid-February 1940. Engine tests were unfortunately awarded low priority, for the bomber was

(Right) The He 177 V7 and (below) the He 177 V6, both of which were evaluated at Bordeaux-Mérignac by IV/KG 40 in the summer of 1941

suffering even more serious aerodynamic troubles. Like the He 177 V2, the V3 carried four crew members whereas the He 177 V1 had provision for a crew of three. Loaded weight was increased to 53,197 lb., wing loading rising from 48.99 lb./sq. ft. to 49.42 lb./sq. ft.

The He 177 V4 (CB-RP), *Werk-Nr*.00 004, was retained at Heinkel's test field where another Rechlin pilot, Ursinus, undertook stability trials. While flying over the Baltic during the course of one of these trials, the He 177 V4 failed to recover from a shallow dive, crashing into the sea near Ribnitz. Attempts to salvage the wreckage in order to determine the cause of the crash met with only partial success, but it was nevertheless discovered that the accident had resulted from the malfunctioning of the airscrew pitch control. The He 177 V4 embodied further weight increases, empty and loaded weights being raised to 31,350 lb. and 54,719 lb. respectively.

Among the He 177's noteworthy features were its Fowler-type extensible trailing-edge flaps which occupied the entire wing trailing edges, including those portions covered by the ailerons. Each aileron comprised upper and lower portions, the latter arranged to slide rearwards with flap extension while the upper part retained its function of providing lateral control for take-off and landing. The original wing design did not take into full account the stresses resulting from operation of the Fowler flaps and thus more internal strengthening proved necessary.

The first four prototypes were essentially similar, apart from the twin bomb-bays installed in the He 177 V2 and the increased internal fuel tankage of the He 177 V4, but the fifth machine, the He 177 V5 (PM-OD), *Werk-Nr*.00 005, and last of the initial prototype batch, incorporated a number of changes which were principally concerned with armament installations for *E-Stelle* Rechlin trials.

Triple bomb-bays were fitted, and hand-operated 7.9-mm. MG 15 machine guns supplanted the 13-mm. MG 131s in the extreme nose of the fuselage, the nose of the gondola and the extreme tail, while a similar weapon was mounted in a turret immediately aft of the flight deck. Early in 1941, during a simulated low-level attack, both DB 606 engines were to burst into flames, the aircraft hitting the ground and exploding.

The tendency on the part of the coupled engines to ignite became increasingly serious as the test programme progressed. There were several reasons for the inflammability of the DB 606, one of which was the common exhaust manifold on the two inner cylinder blocks which became excessively hot and caused the usual accumulation of oil and grease in the bottom of the engine cowling to catch fire. When the pilot throttled back there was a tendency for the injection pump to deliver more fuel than was required by the engine, in addition to which the injection pump connections leaked. In order to restrict weight, no firewall had been provided, and the power plant was fitted so close to the mainspar that there was insufficient space for the fuel and oil pipelines, electrical leads, etc. This "sardine can" arrangement, as it was dubbed at Rechlin, was frequently saturated by fuel and oil from leaking connections. Furthermore, at altitude the oil tended to foam, partly as a result of the return pump being too large, and in this condition it circulated in the engines, its lubricative qualities being reduced virtually to nil. The lack of adequate lubrication resulted in disintegration of the connecting rod bearings which burst through the engine crankcase, puncturing the oil tanks which poured their contents on to the red hot exhaust pipe collector.

Each successive prototype was heavier than its predecessor, and the weights of the He 177

(*Above and right*) *The He 177A-02, the second pre-production aircraft, built at Rostock-Marienehe and flown late in 1941*

V6 (BC-BP), *Werk-Nr*.00 006, had risen to 37,038 lb. in empty equipped condition, and 61,883 lb. loaded, wing loading having risen some 15 per cent to 57.49 lb./sq. ft. However, this was accompanied by a slight increase in power for take-off from 2,600 to 2,700 h.p. which was offered by the production-type DB 606A-1/B-1 (A-1 port and B-1 starboard) engines, these having a maximum continuous rating of 2,360 h.p., and providing a maximum cruising output of 2,080 h.p. at 18,050 ft.

These production-type engines were installed in both the V5 and V6, the performances of these aircraft including maximum and minimum cruising speeds of 289 m.p.h. and 263 m.p.h. respectively, a service ceiling of 22,966 ft., and ranges of 3,355 miles for the He 177 V5 and 3,417 miles for the He 177 V6.

The He 177 V6 and the basically similar **He 177 V7** (SF-TB), *Werk-Nr*.00 007, featured a revised nose section which, while generally following the contours of the nose section

employed by previous prototypes, was considerably reinforced and embodied fewer glazed panels. Whereas the V6 had a 13-mm. MG 131 machine gun in the forward part of the ventral gondola, and similar weapons in the dorsal and tail positions, the V7 had an MG 131 in the fuselage nose, and a 20-mm. MG FF cannon in both the gondola and the dorsal turret.

From the earliest months of the war, *Kampfgeschwader* 40 had been designated the first unit to re-equip with the new bomber, and on August 2, 1941, IV/KG 40 based on Bordeaux-Mérignac received the He 177 V6

and V7 for operational evaluation in the anti-shipping role. The fourth *Gruppe* of each *Geschwader* was, at this stage of the war, a training and replacement unit, and IV/KG 40 was later to be devoted entirely to the development of the He 177 and the training of personnel for this bomber, and was to be re-designated *Ergänzungs/Kampfgruppe He 177*. These two prototypes were soon the bane of all concerned at Bordeaux-Mérignac and, subjected to interminable modifications to both airframes and engines, were declared totally unsuited for operational use.

The He 177 V7 was, incidentally, the first aircraft in the series to feature a reduction in overall length from 67 ft. 6½ in. to 66 ft. 11 in., this slightly shorter fuselage being retained by the pre-production He 177A-0 and the initial production model, the He 177A-1.

In September 1941, the He 177 V8, the last of the aircraft to be built as prototypes from the outset, was made available for engine tests at Rechlin, but owing to the urgency of other development work it was returned to Heinkel after only 40 days, and it was not possible to resume engine tests in the air until February 1942 and the availability of the second pre-production machine, the He 177A-02. The He 177 V8 (SF-TC), *Werk-Nr*.00 008, embodied still further weight increases, empty equipped weight rising to 37,942 lb. and loaded weight to 61,531 lb. Defensive armament reverted to the 7·9-mm. MG 15 in all positions except the extreme tail which retained its 13-mm. MG 131. All sixteen additional *Versuchs* aircraft that followed the He 177 V8 were conversions of pre-production or production airframes.

PRODUCTION VARIANTS

A batch of 15 **He 177A-0** pre-production bombers had been started at Rostock-Marienehe late in 1940, and the first of these, the He 177A-01 (DL-AP), *Werk-Nr*.00 016, was flown in November 1941. Owing to the limited capacity of the Rostock-Marienehe plant, a further 15 pre-production aircraft (*Werk-Nrs*.32 001 to 015) had been laid down simultaneously at Heinkel's Oranienburg factory, and Arado's Warnemünde factory initiated licence production of the bomber with a further five He 177A-0s (*Werk-Nrs*.05 001 to 005).

The He 177A-0 had empty equipped and maximum loaded weights of 37,479 lb. and 66,139 lb. respectively, and as for the He 177 V8, the crew complement was increased to five members. Maximum bomb load was 5,290 lb., and defensive armament comprised one 7.9-mm. MG 81 machine gun on a flexible mounting in the glazed nose, a 20-mm. MG FF cannon in the nose of the ventral gondola, twin aft-firing MG 81 machine guns in the rear of the ventral gondola, a 13-mm. MG 131 machine gun in the dorsal turret and a similar weapon in the extreme tail.

The He 177A-01 was intended primarily for armament tests, and initial trials indicated that the defensive system was unsatisfactory, but before modifications could be introduced the aircraft was destroyed when both power plants caught fire during take-off. The second pre-production machine, the He 177A-02 (DL-AQ), *Werk-Nr*.00 020, began engine flight trials on February 8, 1942, but a few weeks later, in May, both power plants ignited, necessitating a crash landing from which the crew escaped seconds before the plane exploded.

Tests with the He 177A-02 completed prior to its destruction had enabled the engine specialists to reach certain conclusions, however, and they recommended that the engine mountings be lengthened by some eight inches; the fuel and oil pipelines be relocated; a firewall be introduced; the oil tank be transferred to a less dangerous position, and the complete redesign of the exhaust system be undertaken. By this time, the first production He 177A-1 (*Werk-Nr*.15 151) had left Arado's Warnemünde assembly line, and the OKL was demanding the service introduction of the bomber at the earliest possible date. Thus, only the recommendation that the oil tank be shifted was adopted as this change was thought unlikely to delay production. At a later stage, however, when service units began demanding exhaust flame dampers for night operations, the opportunity was taken to redesign the exhaust system, and with the introduction of the He 177A-3 on the assembly line the engine mounts were lengthened by the recommended amount.

Of the 35 He 177A-0 pre-production aircraft, most of those manufactured by the parent company's plant at Oranienburg, which, together with Arado's Warnemünde plant, had been selected as a primary manufacturing centre for the new bomber, were delivered to Ludwigslust for conversion training The remainder were employed for a variety of test programmes, several being allocated *Versuchs* numbers. For example, the He 177A-05 (DL-AT), *Werk-Nr.*00 023, became the He 177 V9, and the He 177A-06 and -07 (DL-AU and -AV) became the V10 and the V11 respectively. The first of the five Warnemünde-built He 177A-0s was used for shallow diving trials at Ludwigslust during which a speed of 443 m.p.h. was attained. This was destined to be the last aircraft to be fitted with the barred-gate type dive brakes for, apart from the fact that the He 177 had proved itself incapable of withstanding the stresses imposed by the pull-out from even a medium-angle dive, Allied anti-aircraft gunners had at last taken the measure of the dive bomber.

The He 177 was still considered to be "dangerous" owing to the frequency with which engine fires occurred, but most experienced bomber pilots expressed favourable opinions concerning its handling qualities and general performance, although take-off characteristics were less favourable, the bomber tending to swing badly, resulting in numerous take-off accidents and necessitating the enlarging of the vertical tail surfaces and provision of a reinforced lateral damper for the tailwheel. These changes eased but failed to eradicate the problem, and it remained necessary to hold the tail down as long as possible during take-off.

Arado's Warnemünde plant, which had completed tooling up for the new bomber and had begun production before Heinkel's Oranienburg factory got into its stride, was solely responsible for manufacture of the He 177A-1 version, for which complete tail assemblies and some fuselage assemblies were produced at Mielec in Poland, and deliveries commenced in March 1942. Arado was to

---

HEINKEL HE 177A-1/R1 GREIF SPECIFICATION

Type: *Five-seat Heavy Bomber.* **Power Plants:** *Two Daimler-Benz DB 606 24-cylinder liquid-cooled engines each rated at 2,700 h.p. for take-off and 2,360 h.p. at 19,030 ft.* **Armament:** *(Defensive) One 7.9-mm. MG 81J machine gun with 2,000 rounds on spherical mounting in glazed nose, one 20-mm. MG FF cannon with 300 rounds in forward ventral gondola position, two 7.9-mm. MG 81 machine guns with 2,000 r.p.g. in aft forward ventral gondola position, one 13-mm. MG 131 machine gun with 750 rounds in remotely-controlled electrically-operated forward dorsal barbette, and one gimbal-mounted 13-mm. MG 131 machine gun with 1,500 rounds in tail position. (Offensive) Short range: 48 110-lb. SC 50, 12 551-lb. SC 250, six 1,102-lb. SC 500 or four 2,205-lb. SC 1000 demolition bombs, six 1,102-lb. SD 500 or six 2,205-lb. SD 1000 armour-piercing bombs, or two 2,205-lb. SD 1000 and two 3,968-lb. SC 1800 bombs, or two LMA III mines plus two 3,968-lb. SC 1800 bombs. Medium range: 32 110-lb. SC 50, eight 551-lb. SC 250, four 1,102-lb. SC or SD 500, or four 2,205-lb. SD 1000 bombs, or four LMA III mines. Long range: 16 110-lb. SC 50, four 551-lb. SC 250, two SC or SD 500, or two 2,205-lb. SD 1000 bombs.* **Performance:** *Maximum speed, 317 m.p.h. at 19,030 ft.; cruising speed, 267 m.p.h. at 18,050 ft.; range (with maximum offensive load and 1,962 Imp. gal. fuel), 745 mls., (with 2,291 Imp. gal.), 1,988 mls., (with 2,820 Imp. gal.), 3,480 mls.; service ceiling, 19,685 ft.* **Weights:** *Empty, 35,494 lb.; empty equipped, 39,771 lb.; maximum loaded, 66,139 lb.* **Dimensions:** *Span, 103 ft. 1¾ in.; length, 66 ft. 11 in.; height, 20 ft. 11¾ in.; wing area, 1,097.918 sq. ft.*

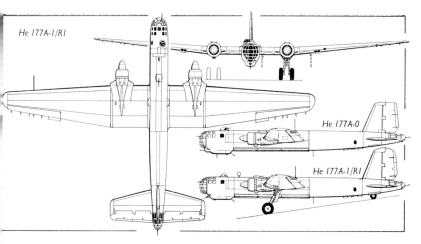

He 177A-1/R1

He 177A-0

He 177A-1/R1

manufacture a total of 130 examples of the He 177A-1, the last of which leaving the assembly line in June 1943.

The He 177A-1 was produced with various armament sets, or *Rüstsätze*, which augmented the standard defensive armament comprising a hand-held 7.9-mm. MG 81 on a small spherical mounting in the glazed nose, a 20-mm. MG FF cannon in the forward end of the nose gondola, an electrically-operated dorsal barbette with a single 13-mm. MG 131 machine gun controlled remotely by a gunner from a sighting station in the roof aft of the pilot, and a single gimbal-mounted MG 131 for the rear gunner who lay prone in the extreme tail. With a supplementary pair of aft-firing 7.9-mm. MG 81 machine guns in the rear of the gondola, the bomber was known

as the **He 177A-1/R1**, this position being used as a sighting station by the **He 177A-1/R2** and **R3** for a remotely-controlled ventral barbette housing a single 13-mm. MG 131, while the **He 177A-1/R4** featured an aft-firing MG 131 in the rear of the ventral gondola plus a manned aft dorsal turret containing a similar weapon.

Despite the considerable background of test and development, the He 177A-1 nevertheless proved unacceptable for operational use, the difficulties with the power plants being compounded by structural problems. A Rechlin report dated October 9, 1942 states: "The examination has shown that the strength of the He 177's wings is one-third below that estimated by Heinkel. The reason for this is the uneven rigidity of the individual members with consequent deformation under load. This condition was not recognised by Heinkel at the proper time, the failure tests having been undertaken too late in view of the size of the structure." The official minutes of a *Generalluftzeugmeister* meeting held a week later included the comment: "He (Heinkel) is aware of the difficulties (experienced with the He 177). He has also recognised that the most important fault lies in the fact that his Technical Bureau has not carried out sufficient fundamental work to take up and carry out necessary modifications." Thus, in November 1942, Dipl.Ing. Hertel returned to Heinkel as an RLM Deputy with full powers to re-organise the development of the He 177.

Within a week of the 130th and last He 177A-1 leaving the Warnemünde line a disposition report revealed that 20 were at Brandenburg-Briest, 12 were at Fassberg, seven at Lechfeld, 19 were at Ludwigslust, 25 were at Lüneburg, 14 were at the repair depot at Eger and another six at the repair depot at Erfurt, although three of those at the latter depot were being used on special long-range reconnaissance missions by Theodore Rowehl's unit, a part of the *Versuchsverbänd Ob.d.L.*, one was with the Junkers plant at Dessau where it was serving as a DB 610 engine test-bed for the Ju 288 programme, six were distributed at various test centres and the remaining 19 had been written off.

While production of the He 177A-1 had been proceeding at Warnemünde, production had begun at Oranienburg of an improved version, the **He 177A-3**. This differed from its predecessor principally in having the power plants mounted some inches further ahead of the wing mainspar, and an additional 5 ft. 3 in. section inserted in the fuselage aft of the bomb-bays. An additional dorsal turret was mounted midway between the trailing edge of the mainplane and the

leading edge of the tailplane, this bein electrically-rotated and hand-elevated, an containing a pair of 13-mm. MG 131 machin guns with 750 r.p.g.

The prototypes for the 177A-3 were th **He 177 V15 and V16** which lacked the add tional aft fuselage section and were powere by DB 610 engines. The DB 610 comprised pair of DB 605 engines and gave a maximu output of 2,950 h.p. for take-off and 3,100 h. at 6,890 ft., and it was proposed that th production He 177A-3 would receive thes more powerful units. However, productic delays frustrated this plan, and thus the ne version of the bomber retained the DB 60 The initial production variant, the **He 177A-R1**, left the Oranienburg assembly line in th late autumn of 1942, but only about a doze examples had been delivered by the end of th year, these going to Brandenburg-Briest f service testing. A delivery tempo of 70 aircra per month had been called for, but owing the continual modifications demanded, t Oranienburg plant had difficulty in deliverin *five* per month before the beginning of 194

In April 1943, an improved variant, t **He 177A-3/R2**, was introduced. This embodie an improved electrical system, a modifie gun position in the nose of the ventral gondo the MG FF cannon being supplanted by MG 151 of similar calibre, and a redesigne tail gun position. Prior to the introduction the He 177A-3/R2, the tail gunner lay pro but the new position enabled the tail gunn to be seated, and his 13-mm. MG 131 w replaced by a 20-mm. MG 151 cannon. T **He 177A-3/R3** was the first Henschel Hs 2 missile carrier, two of these weapons bei mounted beneath the outboard wing pane and one beneath the fuselage, and the **177A-3/R4** had the ventral gondola lengthen by 3 ft. 11 in. to provide more space for t FuG 203b *Kehl III* control transmitter for t

*(Right) An He 177A-3
operated by Kampf-
geschwader 40*

Hs 293 and the *Knüppel* or joystick control box manipulated by the bombardier for line-of-sight guidance. The first tests with the Hs 293 had been made in 1941 with an He 177A-0 at Karlshagen, and subsequently two He 177A-1s were used for further trials at Peenemünde, these effecting the first successful dropping trials in the summer of 1942. The He 177A-3/R3 was used primarily for the training of crews with the Hs 293 from May 1943.

Earlier, during the winter of 1942–43 when He 177s had been hurriedly pressed into service in an attempt to relieve the beleaguered German garrison at Stalingrad, a forward maintenance unit had modified several machines by installing a 50-mm. BK 5 anti-tank gun in the ventral gondola, the ammunition for the gun being housed in the forward bomb-bay, and the modified aircraft being used with some success for ground attack in between transport sorties. Subsequently, the He 177A-3/R5, or *Stalingradtyp*, was evolved, this having a 75-mm. BK 7.5 cannon installed in the gondola, and DB 610 engines in place of the standard DB 606s. Only five machines of this type were completed, however, as the firing of the cannon severely strained the

structure and its installation adversely affected the flying characteristics.

By 1943, Allied advances in anti-submarine warfare were rendering the operation of U-boats in British coastal waters increasingly suicidal, and Admiral Dönitz was particularly insistent that the He 177 be supplied as a torpedo-bomber. Thus, the **He 177A-3/R7** was evolved specifically for the torpedo-bombing role, and was used for trials by *Kampfgeschwader* 26. Initially the Italian L 5 torpedo, standard with *Luftwaffe* torpedo-bombing units, was used, but these weapons, with their jettisonable stabilizing extensions, could not be stowed in the He 177's bomb-bays, and thus two torpedoes were carried beneath the fuselage and, subsequently, beneath the wings. Unlike its predecessors, the He 177A-3/R7 had no Fowler-type flaps along the ailerons, the outer wings being similar to those of the later He 177A-5, and this variant was also used for trials with the new electrically-driven LT 50 torpedo which could be dropped by parachute from an altitude of some 800 ft. at a considerable distance from its target. However, only three examples of the He 177A-3/R7 were produced, this variant being abandoned in favour of the **He 177A-5**.

With the completion of 170 He 177A-3s both the Oranienburg and Warnemünde plants switched completely to production of the He 177A-5, the first example of which had left the former factory in February 1943, the combined delivery rate of the two facilities attaining 12 per month by July and 42 per month by the end of the year, a total of 261 having been completed by the end of 1943 when the RLM, prompted presumably by the high attrition, issued instructions that all existing He 177 bombers were to be scrapped!

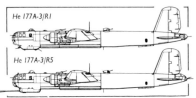

He 177A-3/R1

He 177A-3/R5

Meanwhile, the engine test section at the *Erprobungsstelle* Rechlin had modified one machine to conform with recommendations resulting from the findings of the investigation team ordered by Dipl.Ing. Hertel in January 1943 to ascertain all possible sources of engine fires. This investigation had revealed 56 possible causes of fire, and the machine modified at Rechlin functioned perfectly, the engines giving no trouble whatsoever over a protracted test period. The *Technische Amt* was finally convinced that the solution to the He 177's engine troubles had at last been found, but the order to modify all aircraft on the assembly lines in a similar fashion came too late as it would have seriously disrupted production deliveries, while the order to scrap existing machines was tacitly ignored.

The He 177A-5 was intended primarily to carry external loads, such as the LT 5 torpedo, the FX 1400 *Fritz X* and the Hs 293. It standardized on the DB 610 engine, embodied a strengthened wing, shortened undercarriage oleo legs, and the Fowler flaps along the outboard wing sections were removed. The defensive armament stemmed from that of the He 177A-3/R2, and thus the standard production variant was designated **He 177A-5/R2**. The triple bomb-bay was installed, but the forward bay was blanked off and a ventral weapon rack was fitted.

Several sub-types of the He 177A-5 were produced, these including the **He 177A-5/R** which had an additional remotely-controlled gun barbette positioned aft of the bomb-bays, only one example of this version being completed; the **He 177A-5/R6** which was essentially similar to the R5 apart from the deletion of the two forward bomb-bays; the **He 177A-5/R7** which featured a pressurized cabin enabling a ceiling of 49,870 ft. to be attained, and the **He 177A-5/R8**, the sole example of which was equipped with remotely controlled "chin" and tail barbettes but was abandoned as a result of difficulties with the barbette control system.

During 1944, a total of 565 He 177A-5s was completed, although the entire production programme virtually ground to a halt during October in favour of the "emergency fighter programme".

OPERATIONAL CAREER

As mentioned earlier, the OKL had envisaged *Kampfgeschwader* 40 as the first He 177-equipped unit, and as early as the summer of 1941, IV/KG 40 based at Bordeaux-Mérignac had evaluated the He 177 V6 and V7, but more than a year elapsed before 1.*Staffel* began conversion on the He 177A-1 at Fassberg.

HEINKEL HE 177A-5/R2 GREIF SPECIFICATION

Type: *Six-Seat Heavy Bomber, Reconnaissance and Anti-Shipping Aircraft.* **Power Plants:** *Two Daimler-Benz DB 610A-1/B-1 (A-1 port and B-1 starboard) 24-cylinder liquid-cooled engines each rated at 2,950 h.p for take-off and 3,100 h.p. at 6,890 ft.* **Armament:** *(Defensive) One 7.9-mm. MG 81J machine gun with 2,000 rounds on spherical mounting in glazed nose, one 20-mm. MG 151 cannon with 300 rounds in forward ventral gondola position, two 7.9-mm. machine guns with 2,000 r.p.g. in rear ventral gondola position, two 13-mm. MG 131 machine guns with 750 r.p.g. in remotely-controlled forward dorsal barbette, one 13-mm. MG 131 machine gun with 750 rounds in electrically-operated aft dorsal turret and one 20-mm. MG 151 cannon with 300 rounds in tail position. (Offensive) Internally: 16 110-lb. SC 50, four 551-lb. SC 250 or two 1,102-lb. SC 500 general-purpose bombs. Externally: Two LMA III parachute sea mines, LT 50 torpedoes, two Henschel Hs 293 or FX 1400 Fritz X missiles.* **Performance:** *Maximum speed (at 59,966 lb.), 303 m.p.h. at 20,000 ft., 248 m.p.h. at sea level, (at 68,343 lb.), 273 m.p.h. at 20,000 ft.; maximum cruising speed, 258 m.p.h. at 20,000 ft.; economical cruising speed, 210 m.p.h. at 20,000 ft.; maximum range with two Hs 293 missiles, 3,417 mls., with two Fritz X missiles, 3,100 mls.; initial climb rate, 620 ft./min.; to 10,000 ft., 10 mins., to 20,000 ft., 39 min.; service ceiling, 26,250 ft.* **Weights:** *Empty equipped, 37,038 lb.; normal loaded, 59,966 lb.; maximum, 68,343 lb.* **Dimensions:** *Span, 103 ft. 1¾ in.; length, 72 ft. 2 in.; height, 20 ft. 11¾ in.; wing area, 1,097.918 sq. ft.*

he meantime, I/KG 4, which had been perating He 111s on the Russian Front until ne autumn of 1942, was withdrawn to echfeld where 3.*Staffel* began conversion to he He 177A-1, 2. and 3.*Staffeln* subsequently eing formed with crews drawn from KG 4's ther *Gruppen*, and late in 1942, I/KG 50 was ormed at Brandenburg-Briest from a cadre f KG 40's 10.*Staffel.* I/KG 50 was specifically ntended to take the He 177 into service on the ussian Front, and after conversion on 20 e 177A-1s at Brandenburg-Briest, was ushed to Zaparozhe for winter trials with the rst He 177A-3/R1s under *Luftflotte* 4.

The worsening situation of the 6th Army in talingrad at the turn of the year called for an ll-out effort on the part of the *Luftwaffe* to ount an effective airlift, and the He 177s of KG 50 were promptly applied to the trans-ort role, although only seven aircraft were

serviceable at Zaparozhe. On the first opera-tion mounted by these seven aircraft, the *Gruppenkommandeur*, Major Scheede, was lost, and as the He 177 was found to be totally unsuited for the transport role, carrying little more than the appreciably smaller and infinitely more reliable He 111 and being virtually useless for the evacuation of wounded troops, I/KG 50 reverted to bombing missions in support of the *Wehrmacht* in the vicinity of Stalingrad. Only 13 missions were flown and seven of the He 177s crashed in flames without any action attributable to the enemy, and in February 1943, the personnel and surviving aircraft were withdrawn to Brandenburg-Briest.

I/KG 50 was subsequently retrained for the anti-shipping role with the Hs 293 missile, and, on October 25, 1943, this *Gruppe* was re-designated II/KG 40 (in place of the original

*(Left) An He 177A-5 serving with Kampfgeschwader 100 during the winter of 1943-4

Do 217-equipped II/KG 40 which had now become V/KG 2) and was transferred from Burg-Magdeburg to Bordeaux-Mérignac for operations over the Atlantic. The first major operation flown by II/KG 40 took place on November 21, 1943, when, under the control of the *Fliegerführer Atlantik*, 20 Hs 293-carrying He 177A-5s attacked the 66-ship convoy SL.139/MKS.30 en route to Britain from Sierra Leone (SL.139) and North Africa (MKS.30). The convoy had been harried without result by over 30 U-boats, and the *Fliegerführer Atlantik* launched II/KG 40, despite poor visibility, in desperation. Only 16 Hs 293 missiles were seen to be released, a number of these being aimed against a straggler three-and-a-half miles behind the main body of the convoy. The straggler was finally hit and abandoned, but only one other merchantman was damaged, and three of the He 177s were destroyed. Five days later, II/KG 40 again went into action against an

Allied convoy off Bougie, but four of the 1 Hs 293-carrying aircraft were lost in action and three more were written-off after force landings. Thus, 50 per cent of the attacking force was lost in this one action, casualtie including the *Gruppenkommandeur*, Majo Mons, and II/KG 40 was left with only seve serviceable aircraft.

The heavy losses sustained indicated tha daylight attacks with the He 177 agains convoys were impracticable, and it wa concluded that attacks on shipping would hav to be carried out at night, either with the ai of bright moonlight or with flares. Ne tactics were therefore evolved, one *Kette* aircraft dropping special 110-lb. flares on th beam of the convoy while another *Kett* attacked from the dark side, seeing its targe silhouetted against the light of the flares. A the He 177s were less vulnerable to anti aircraft fire in the darkness, they released the Hs 293s from a range of six to nine mile

158

while flying directly towards their target, thus greatly simplifying the problem of aiming.

Meanwhile, I/KG 40 had begun conversion to the He 177 at Fassberg early in 1943, although progress was slow owing to the shortage of aircraft—from March until the beginning of September only three serviceable He 177A-1s were available—and 1.*Staffel* eventually arrived at Chateaudun on December 19, 1943, together with half of 2.*Staffel* (the former 8./KG 40), the other half of the latter *Staffel* remaining at Fassberg to complete its training. At Chateaudun, the elements of I/KG 40 joined the similarly-equipped ./KG 100 which had arrived from Lechfeld on the previous day. I/KG 4, which had been trained from the outset as a bomber rather than anti-shipping unit, had been redesignated I/KG 100 on October 1, 1943, and while 3.*Staffel* transferred to Chateaudun, 1. and 2.*Staffeln* remained at Lechfeld to complete their training.

For operation *Steinbock*, the so-called "Little Blitz" which was to mark the début of the He 177 over the British Isles, 1./KG 40 and 3./KG 100 came under *Fliegerkorps IX* and were co-ordinated as a single unit. Operation *Steinbock* had been conceived on the direct orders of Adolf Hitler as a reprisal against London, the OKL being forced to comb every operational unit in Italy and Russia for bombers to participate, some 550 aircraft

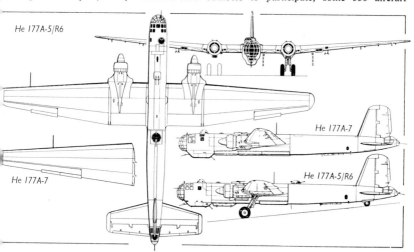

He 177A-5/R6

He 177A-7

He 177A-7

He 177A-5/R6

eventually being gathered together, of which 35 were the He 177s from KG 40 and KG 100. In the first *Steinbock* attack against London on January 21, 1944, an attack which fell far short of the OKL's expectations as a mere 30 tons of bombs fell over the Greater London area as compared with 270 tons scattered elsewhere, the He 177A-5s of 1./KG 40 and 3./KG 100 took-off from Chateaudun and returned to Rheine. After two more attacks on London from the latter base, 1./KG 40 was withdrawn to Fassberg and replaced by 2./KG 100 which had, in the meantime, attained operational status, reaching Chateaudun on February 4th.

While, as an operation, *Steinbock* could only be considered an abysmal failure, the He 177s achieved some successes. The more experienced crews carried maximum bomb loads and, climbing to 23,000 ft. while still over German territory, approached their target in a shallow dive, attaining speeds in excess of 430 m.p.h. at which night fighters could not intercept them and anti-aircraft fire could not follow them. In this way, only four He 177s were lost to enemy action, but, nevertheless, a very low degree of concentration was attained, and serviceability was invariably low as a result of last-minute mishaps before operations. Evidence of this was provided Major-General Pelz, who had been appointed *Angriffsführer England* by Göring, when, on the night of February 13th, he witnessed the take-off and landing at Rheine of 2. and 3.*Staffeln* of KG 100. It was a cold night and the "cold start" procedure was employed. Thirteen aircraft took-off—one having come to grief with a burst tyre—but eight of these promptly returned to base with overheated or burning engines. Of the remaining five, only four reached London, the *Gruppenkommandeur*, finding himself over Norwich, had turned back, dumping his bombs in the Zuyder Zee.

Of the four He 177s which did reach London one was shot down by night fighters. By the end of February, 1./KG 100 had reached Chateaudun to complete the *Gruppe*, but at the beginning of March *Steinbock* was called off.

In January 1944, the He 177s of II/KG 40 at Bordeaux-Mérignac had been transferred to the command of *Luftflotte* 2 to help combat Allied landings at Anzio, and on the 23rd of that month seven He 177s, each with two Hs 293 missiles and 16 110-lb. flares, took-off for a dusk attack on shipping in the area of the Nettuno beach-head which proved abortive. On the following day, 11 aircraft of the *Gruppe* took-off from Bordeaux-Mérignac to repeat the operation, again without positive results, and shortly afterwards II/KG 40 reverted to Atlantic reconnaissance, operational strength having fallen from 18 to six aircraft. In February 1944, 3./KG 40, its strength built up to 15 aircraft, was transferred to northern Norway under the *Fliegerführer Nordmeer*, replacing the Fw 200-equipped *Staffel* at Trondheim-Vaernes.

As the year 1944 progressed, He 177 operations became increasingly desultory. Fuel and personnel shortages presented insurmountable difficulties, and He 177s were sitting on airfields all over Europe awaiting the replacement of engines and other modifications. With the disbanding of KG 40, the He 177 finally disappeared from the anti-shipping role, although as late as September 1944, He 177s were being converted as Hs 293 missile carriers, and the *Versuchskommando* of *Kampfgeschwader* 200 continued to use a few aircraft of this type until the early months of 1945.

CONTINUED DEVELOPMENT

While production of the He 177A-5 had proceeded, several derivatives of the basi

*(Above) An He 177
A-5/R2 and (right) an
FX 1400 Fritz X mount-
ed beneath the blanked-
off forward bomb-bay*

design had been evolved, including the **He 177A-6**. Work on this extensively revised model had begun early in 1944, and preparations had been made to switch production from the He 177A-5 to the newer variant immediately. The constant flow of modifications resulting from the complaints of front-line units delayed plans, however, and instead of 15 He 177A-6s ready for delivery by the end of May 1944, only six were actually completed

and their assembly was possible only by utilising 98 per cent A-5 components. Indeed, the first six **He 177A-6/R1** long-range heavy bombers were conversions of He 177A-5/R6 aircraft and featured pressure cabins. The rear dorsal turret was deleted as an electrically-operated Rheinmetall-Borsig turret with four 7.9-mm. MG 81 machine guns was mounted in the extreme tail, this being considered to provide adequate rear defence. The two forward bomb-bays were deleted, and the rear bay could accommodate a 1,100-lb. load but the principal offensive load (5,500 lb.) was carried beneath the fuselage. Maximum range was 3,600 miles, and the fuel cells were heavily armoured.

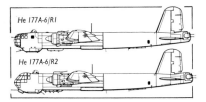

He 177A-6/R1

He 177A-6/R2

The seventh He 177A-6 was designated **He 177 V22** and was intended as a prototype for the **He 177A-6/R2** which differed from the R1 principally in having an entirely redesigned fuselage nose of improved aerodynamic form. Defensive armament comprised twin 13-mm. MG 131 machine guns in a "chin" barbette, twin 20-mm. MG 151 cannon in the remotely-controlled forward dorsal barbette, an aft-firing 13-mm. MG 131 in the ventral forward-fuselage step, and a four-gun HDL 81V tail turret. Alternative offensive loads included one 1,102-lb. SC 500 and one 5,512-lb. SC 2500 general-purpose bomb, one 2,205-lb. SC 1000 and one 4,409-lb. SC 2000 general-purpose bomb, two *Fritz X* missiles and one 1,102-lb. SC 500 bomb, or one Hs 293D missile and one SC 500 bomb. After the completion of the He 177 V22, the entire He 177A-6/R2 programme was abandoned in favour of the He 277.

The **He 177A-7** was planned as an high-altitude bomber with an extended wing spanning 118 ft. 1⅓ in. and a pair of DB 613 coupled engines, these each comprising two DB 603Gs and offering 3,600 h.p. for take-off and 3,150 h.p. for climb and combat. To simplify and accelerate construction of this variant of the bomber it was decided to employ standard A-5 airframes, and the six examples of the He 177A-7 completed retained the DB 610 power plants. Empty and loaded weights were increased to 33,913 lb. and 76,280 lb. respectively, and maximum speed was increased to 335 m.p.h. at 20,000 ft.

The Imperial Japanese Navy had begun to evince interest in the He 177 at an early stage in its development, and work was actually initiated on the construction of a factory at Chiba where the bomber was to be licence-manufactured by Hitachi. However, in order to avoid a repetition of the engine fire problems experienced by the *Luftwaffe*, the Imperial Navy model was to have employed four separate air-cooled radial engines. Sample tools had been delivered to Japan by submarine, and the third He 177A-7, completed in May 1944, was offered to Japan for service evaluation and for use as a pattern airframe.

With much of its armour stripped and additional fuel cells installed in the wings and bomb-bays, the aircraft was readied in the summer of 1944 for a non-stop ferry flight from Germany to Japan. Heinkel proposed that this should be made at extreme altitude via Siberia, but the Japanese insisted the aircraft be flown via Persia and India, basing their refusal to permit the aircraft to be flown over the shorter route on their neutrality pact with the Soviet Union, and strangely persisting in this attitude after the Soviet Union had renounced the non-aggression pact. As the He 177A-7 possessed insufficient range to make the non-stop flight over the route proposed by the Japanese, it remained in Germany and, together with the other five aircraft of this type, was to have been used to make suicidal attacks on targets in the U.S.A. In

(Above) The fourth He 177A-7 after capture by U.S. forces. This aircraft was later ferried to the U.S.A. for evaluation purposes. Five other examples of this sub-type were scrapped in the late autumn of 1944

fact, one He 177A-7 *did* reach the U.S.A., this being the fourth machine which, captured by U.S. forces, was later ferried to the United States for test purpose, the five other examples of this type being scrapped in the late autumn of 1944.

An interesting experiment in aerial defence was conducted with the He 177 in the summer of 1944 by the *Versuchs-Jagdgruppe* 10 at Pardubitz. Three He 177s were delivered to this unit in June 1944, and modified for use as bomber "destroyers", their bomb-bays being removed, together with the fuel tanks immediately aft of the cockpit, and a battery of 33 rocket launching tubes installed. The tubes were inclined to fire upward at an angle of 60° to the horizontal axis of the aircraft and slightly to starboard. The upper section of the fuselage in which the tubes were installed was fitted with a cover containing 33 circular holes. For firing control purposes the battery was divided into two groups of 18 and 15 rockets, and a selector switch allowed for the firing of the entire battery in groups or as single projectiles.

After initial trials at Pardubitz, the three He 177 *Zerstörers* were flown to Rechlin for further trials and operational evaluation by VJGr. 10. The intended mode of operation called for the He 177s to follow enemy bomber formations, passing below and to port of the intruders, maintaining a difference of altitude of 6,000 ft. at the time of the attack from below. A few trial daylight operations were flown but no contact was made with Allied bomber formations, and as the American escort fighters were becoming ever more numerous the entire scheme was abandoned.

It has been said that the He 177 *Greif* was deadlier to its crews than to its enemies. This is, of course, an exaggeration, but this bomber, advanced though it was in concept, suffered far more development problems than any of its contemporaries, and these led to its failure; a failure which prevented the *Luftwaffe* maintaining any large-scale strategic bombing offensive. Of ambitious design, it embodied as much ingenuity as any bomber to see combat, but the advances that it offered were nullified by the German aircraft industry's inability to devote sufficient effort towards their perfection.

German interest in bombers capable of operating at altitudes affording them immunity from fighter interception first manifested itself in the mid 'thirties, and it was hardly surprising that at an early stage in the development of the Heinkel He 177 consideration should be given to producing a version which, with pressurized accommodation for the crew, would operate at extreme altitudes. The design of such a variant of the He 177 did, in fact, commence in 1940, and had reached an advanced stage during the early months of 1941, development paralleling that of the He 177A-3 which was, at that time, considered to be the definitive orthodox production version of the bomber.

It was envisaged that the He 177A-3 would receive Daimler-Benz DB 610 coupled units which were scheduled to supplant the lower-powered DB 606s then being installed in the initial production He 177A-1. The DB 610 was also intended to power the high-altitude model, the He 177A-4, which, while retaining the A-3 airframe, was to feature a pressurized compartment for a crew of three, this featuring double walls of heavy-gauge light alloy, hollow-sandwich-type glazing and inflatable rubber seals, a pressure equivalent to that at 8,200 ft. being maintained. Defensive armament was restricted to a single forward-firing 13-mm. MG 131 machine gun and remotely-controlled dorsal and ventral barbettes each containing a pair of MG 131s and directed from a blister in the roof of the flight deck.

As design work on the He 177A-4 progressed at Vienna-Schwechat, it became increasingly obvious to the Heinkel team that the commonality of airframe components with the He 177A-3 demanded by the *Technische Amt*

(Left) The He 274 V1 at Orleans-Bricy during initial flight trials

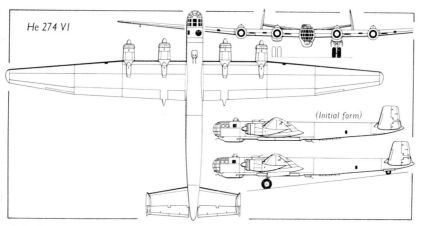

He 274 V1

(Initial form)

of the RLM could not be maintained if the operational ceiling demanded by the *Oberkommando der Luftwaffe* (OKL) was to be attained. Research had revealed the fact that an appreciable reduction in wing loading would have to be accompanied by a very considerable increase in the aspect ratio of the wing, and flexing considerations rendered a simple extension of the existing single-spar wing impracticable. The Heinkel team therefore proposed to the *Technische Amt* that an entirely new long-span wing of two-spar construction and an aspect ratio of 13 be married to the He 177A-4 fuselage. This proposal was accompanied by the suggestion that the newly-developed Heinkel-Hirth 9-2291 (TK 11) exhaust-driven turbo-superchargers be adopted, the use of these dictating the abandoning of the coupled engine arrange-

ment in favour of four independent units.

By mid-1941, Heinkel was engrossed by the task of eradicating the teething troubles suffered by the He 177 prototypes which, coupled with other urgent projects, left the company seriously short of detail design capacity. The *Technische Amt* had finally accepted the proposals concerning the changes considered necessary to produce an effective high-altitude bomber and, in view of the extent of these changes, the RLM had allocated a new type number to the project, and thus, as the He 274, it was decided to transfer detail design and development to the Société Anonyme des Usines Farman (SAUF), an order being placed with the Suresnes plant for two prototypes and four pre-production aircraft.

Design development of the He 274 pro-

165

gressed slowly at the SAUF drawing office in Paris, despite some 250 French draughtsmen being applied to the task under the supervision of Heinkel personnel, and changes were steadily incorporated in the design until little more than a superficial resemblance to the He 177 remained. The fuselage, which, apart from the pressure cabin, was essentially similar to that of the He 177A-3 and possessed an overall length of 64 ft. 3½ in., was lengthened at an early stage to 73 ft. 9 in., and the undercarriage, the main members of which originally comprised two single-wheel oleo legs, one leg retracting inward and the other outward, was rearranged to comprise two twin-wheel main members retracting aft into extended inboard engine nacelles.

Construction of the two prototypes, the **He 274 V1** and **V2**, did not actually commence at Suresnes until 1943 when it was proposed that these aircraft would be powered by DB 603A-2 engines with exhaust-driven TK 11 turbo-superchargers, the pre-production **He 274A-0** bombers having DB 603G engines with both mechanically-driven superchargers and exhaust-driven turbo-superchargers and offering 1,900 h.p. for take-off and 1,450 h.p. at 36,100

ft. In the event, late in 1943, the four pre-production He 274A-0 bombers were cancelled, but work on the prototypes continued.

The wing of the He 274 comprised a two-piece centre section with detachable outer panels built up on two heavy mainspars, with extruded aluminium flanges and sheet webs, forming a box-type girder, the space between the spars being partly occupied by four fuel tanks (two in the centre section and two in the outer panels) with a total capacity of 968 Imp. gal., and the oil tanks for both the engines and the turbo-superchargers. Beneath the centre-section trailing edge were the hydraulically-operated Fowler-type split flaps which were divided into 10 sections, the ailerons, which were controlled by means of servo tabs, being arranged to droop with flap extension.

The fuselage was of orthodox semi-monocoque type, with transverse frames, longitudinal stringers and several longerons, and immediately aft of the pressurized cabin was the main 334 Imp. gal. capacity fuel tank and two bomb-bays. Provision was made for a 425 Imp. gal. long-range tank to replace the bombs in one bay for extended-range missions, and two 224 Imp. gal. auxiliary tanks could be mounted in the rear fuselage to provide an overload fuel capacity of 2,175 Imp. gal. with which a 4,400-lb. bomb load could be carried.

At an early stage in the development of the He 274, the crew complement had been increased to four members, with pilot and co-pilot seated side-by-side and the navigator-bombardier and radio-operator aft, these last two respectively operating the dorsal and ventral FDL 131Z gun barbettes from the glazed sighting dome and a sighting position in the rear of the deepened fuselage nose. During the course of prototype construction at Suresnes yet a further increase was made in the fuselage length, a 4 ft. 3¼ in. section being inserted in the aft fuselage to increase the moment arm for improved control effectiveness simultaneously augmenting directional and longitudinal stability. The decision to lengthen the fuselage was accompanied by the elimination of the servo tabs from the elevators.

The He 274 V1 was being readied for flight testing at Suresnes in July 1944 when the approach of Allied forces necessitated the evacuation of Heinkel personnel working on the project. Minor difficulties had already delayed the initiation of flight testing and the ferrying of the first aircraft to Germany by several weeks, and orders were therefore given to destroy the virtually-completed prototype. Explosive charges were consequently hurriedly attached to each engine, and the German personnel departed, taking with them all works drawings. Fortunately, little damage was done to the airframe of the He 274 V1, and repairs were begun shortly after the liberation, a new set of engines being discovered in another factory, and in December 1945 the first flight test was effected at Orleans-Bricy. In the meantime, the SAUF organisation had been nationalised as the Ateliers Aéronautiques de Suresnes, the He 274 V1 being redesignated AAS 01A. Flight trials continued from Brétigny-sur-Orge, these initially being concerned with cabin pressurization tests, but proposals to complete the He 274 V2 were not to see fruition. The He 274 V1 (alias AAS 01A) subsequently served as a launching aircraft for reduced-scale models of the SO 4000 and NC 270, finally being broken up at Marseilles-Istres late in 1953.

HEINKEL HE 274 SPECIFICATION

Type: *Four-seat High-Altitude Heavy Bomber.* **Power Plants:** *Four Daimler-Benz DB 603A-2 12-cylinder liquid-cooled engines with TK 11B turbo-superchargers each rated at 1,750 h.p. for take-off, 1,850 h.p. at 6,900 ft. and (with TK 11B turbo-superchargers) 1,450 h.p. at 36,100 ft.* **Armament:** *(Proposed) One 13-mm. MG 131 machine gun in fuselage nose, two 13-mm. MG 131 machine guns in remotely-controlled FDL 131Z forward dorsal barbette, and two 13-mm. MG 131 machine guns in remotely-controlled FDL 131Z ventral barbette; (Offensive) Maximum bomb load of 8,820 lb. in two internal bays.* **Performance:** *Maximum speed, 267 m.p.h. at sea level, 304 m.p.h. at 9,840 ft., 360 m.p.h. at 36,090 ft.; cruising speed (75 per cent power) 248 m.p.h. at sea level, 280 m.p.h. at 9,840 ft., 317 m.p.h. at 36,090 ft.; normal range, 1,770 mls. at 283 m.p.h. at 18,700 ft., or 2,137 mls. at 36,090 ft.; maximum range, 2,640 mls. at 36,090 ft.; climb to 6,560 ft., 8.3 min., to 19,685 ft., 32.5 min., to 42,650 ft., 1 hr. 30 min.; maximum ceiling, 46,920 ft.* **Weights:** *empty, 46,958 lb.; empty equipped, 52,558 lb.; loaded, 79,388 lb.; maximum overload, 83,800 lb.* **Dimensions:** *Span, 145 ft. 0 in.; length, 78 ft. 1¼ in.; height (tail up), 18 ft. 0½ in.; wing area, 1,829.86 sq. ft.*

One of the simplest means of solving the power plant difficulties suffered by the He 177 would have been the adoption of four independent engines at a relatively early stage in the development life of the bomber, and Heinkel's project office at Vienna-Schwechat did, in fact, make such proposals to the RLM's *Technische Amt* in 1940. At that time, however, only the first prototypes were flying, and the RLM could not conceive the possibility that the initial difficulties encountered by the coupled engine arrangement might prove insurmountable. Furthermore, the use of four separate power plants had obvious disadvantages from the aerodynamic viewpoint, markedly increasing drag and resulting in inferior powers of manoeuvre.

By the autumn of 1941, the tendency on the part of the coupled engines to ignite was becoming increasingly serious, but while the *Technische Amt* agreed to a switch from coupled engines to four individual power plants for the He 274 pressurized high-altitude bomber as this embodied so much redesign that it no longer possessed any real commonality with the He 177 from which it stemmed, it was adamant in its refusal to countenance the development of the parallel He 277 which made use of standard He 177 airframe components and individual engines. Indeed, continued difficulties with the coupled engines and consequent pressure on the part of Professor Heinkel for the development of this bomber in favour of the He 177 resulted in Hermann Göring expressly forbidding any further mention of the He 277!

Despite this official opposition, Heinkel clandestinely continued the design development of the He 277, and in all correspondence its continued existence was disguised under

The He 277 V1 (below) began flight trials at Vienna-Schwechat late in 1943, but to delude Göring and the RLM it was referred to as the He 177B-0. The He 277 V1 employed a standard He 177A-3/R2 airframe and four DB 603A liquid-cooled engines with annular nose radiators

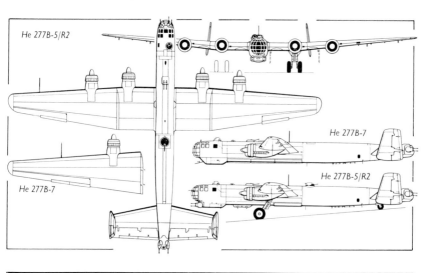

He 277B-5/R2

He 277B-7

He 277B-7

He 277B-5/R2

HEINKEL HE 277B-5/R2 SPECIFICATION

Type: *Seven-seat Heavy Bomber.* **Power Plants:** *Four Daimler-Benz DB 603A 12-cylinder liquid-cooled engines each rated at 1,750 h.p. for take-off and 1,850 h.p. at 6,900 ft.* **Armament:** *(Defensive) One 7.9-mm. MG 81J or 15-mm. or 20-mm. MG 151 cannon on spherical mounting in glazed nose, four 7.9-mm. MG 81 machine guns in remotely-controlled HDL 81V "chin" barbette, two 13-mm. MG 131 machine guns in remotely-controlled forward dorsal FDL 131E/F2 barbette, one 13-mm. MG 131J machine gun in EDL 131A-2 dorsal turret, and four 7.9-mm. MG 81 machine guns in hydraulically-operated HDL 81V tail turret. (Offensive) Internal load of 1,100-lb. bombs plus (externally) two FX 1400 Fritz X missiles, one Henschel Hs 293 or 294 missile, or one 5,512-lb. SC 2500 bomb.* **Performance:** *Maximum speed, 354 m.p.h. at 18,700 ft., 302 m.p.h. at sea level; economical cruising speed, 286 m.p.h. at 17,700 ft.; maximum range, 3,728 mls.; maximum ceiling, 49,210 ft.* **Weights:** *Empty equipped, 48,060 lb.; maximum loaded, 98,105 lb.* **Dimensions:** *Span, 103 ft. 1¾ in.; length, 72 ft. 8 in.; height, 21 ft. 10½ in.; wing area, 1,076.39 sq. ft.*

the spurious designation "He 177B", although all drawings, calculations and works memoranda still referred to the bomber as the He 277, so its *unofficial* development was very much an open secret, but it was not until May 1943 that official sanction for the development of this aircraft was obtained. This came about as a result of a meeting held at Obersalzberg on the 23rd of that month between Adolf Hitler and senior representatives of the aircraft industry. During the course of the meeting, the *Führer* demanded a dual-purpose bomber capable of attacking London by day and night from altitudes at which interceptors would be powerless to intervene, and also suitable for attacking Allied convoys far out in the Atlantic. Heinkel claimed that the "He 177B" would be capable of fulfilling these demands, and was promptly given instructions to proceed immediately with its development.

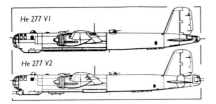

He 277 V1

He 277 V2

A standard He 177A-3/R2 airframe was taken from the assembly line and modified to take four independent Daimler-Benz DB 603A 12-cylinder liquid-cooled engines with annular nose radiators. Designated **He 277 V1** (NN-QQ), the prototype began flight trials at Vienna-Schwechat late in 1943, and to delude Göring and the RLM, which was still opposed to any development that might detract from Heinkel's efforts in solving the production bomber's difficulties, the aircraft was referred

to as the He 177B-0. The second prototype, the **He 277 V2** (GA-QQ), referred to in correspondence between Heinkel and the RLM as the He 177B-5/R1, was a conversion of a standard He 177A-5/R8 airframe, and was flown for the first time on February 28, 1944. This aircraft was initially used primarily for stability trials, small auxiliary fins being added to the tailplane to rectify some directional instability, and in April was ferried to the *Erprobungsstelle* Rechlin for official evaluation.

The **He 277 V3** (KW-TT) was similar to the V2 when initially flown but some vestiges of directional instability remained, and these were finally eradicated by the introduction of an entirely new tail assembly employing twin fins and rudders. Like its immediate predecessor, the V3 was equipped with a defensive armament comprising a remotely-controlled Rheinmetall-Borsig "chin" barbette housing a battery of four 7.9-mm. MG 81 machine guns, a similar armament in a manned tail turret, a single 7.9-mm. MG 81 in the glazed nose, a pair of 13-mm. MG 131 machine guns in the remotely-controlled forward dorsal barbette, and a single MG 131 in the rear dorsal turret.

After a conference held on May 25, 1944, Göring, declaring that the heavy bomber remained "the kernel of aerial armament", ordered the immediate quantity production of the He 277B, the aim being a delivery rate of no fewer than 200 machines per month! The initial production model was the **He 277B-5/R2** intended for heavy bomber operation over medium and long ranges and powered by four 1,750 h.p. DB 603A engines, but at that stage of the conflict Göring's order was anything but realistic, and on July 3, 1944, the entire bomber programme was abandoned in favour of the "emergency fighter programme", and only eight production He 277s were completed of which two or three were flown before all completed aircraft and those still on the assembly line were scrapped.

Prior to the termination of all bomber development, work had started on two further variants, the **He 277B-6** and **B-7**. The He 277B-6 had a wing span increased to 131 ft. 2¾ in. and four 2,060 h.p. Junkers Jumo 213F 12-cylinder liquid-cooled engines. Other changes included an increase in the dihedral angle of the tailplane and enlarged endplate fins and rudders. The **He 277B-6/R1** was to have employed the Rheinmetall-Borsig HL/ 131V hydraulically-operated tail turret housing four 13-mm. MG 131 machine guns. This turret was heavily armoured and, in view of some of its features, it was fortunate for *Luftwaffe* tail gunners that it never attained operational service. In the event of the hydraulic elevation drive failing, the top of the gunner's control stick had to be unscrewed and removed before the handle for emergency operation could be turned; the emergency firing switch had to be operated by the gunner's *left knee*, and the turret door was hinged at the bottom and, after locking, could only be opened in *level* flight, an attitude unlikely to be adopted by the gunner at the moment the gunner wanted to bale out! Other defensive armament comprised twin 20-mm.

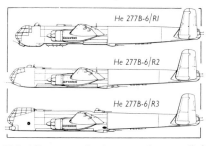

MG 151 cannon in the remotely-controlled "chin" barbette, and a pair of similar weapons in dorsal and ventral barbettes.

The **He 277B-6/R2** had the width of its fuselage reduced from 6 ft. 3 in. to 4 ft. 11 in., the bomb-bay shortened and deepened,

---

HEINKEL HE 277B-6/R1 SPECIFICATION

Type: *Six-seat Heavy Bomber, Reconnaissance and Anti-Shipping Aircraft.* **Power Plants:** *Four Junkers Jumo 213F 12-cylinder liquid-cooled engines (with MW 50 methanol-water injection) each rated at 2,060 h.p. for take-off and 2,040 h.p. at 5,600 ft.* **Armament:** *(Defensive) Twin 20-mm. MG 151 cannon in remotely-controlled FDL 151Z "chin" barbette, twin 20-mm. MG 151 cannon in remotely-controlled FDL 151Z forward dorsal barbette, twin 20-mm. MG 151 cannon in FDL 151Z ventral barbette and four 13-mm. MG 131 machine guns in hydraulically-operated HDL 131V tail turret. (Offensive) Internal load of 1,100-lb. bombs plus (externally) one 5,512-lb. SC 2500 bomb, one Henschel Hs 293 or 294 missile or two FX 1400 Fritz X missiles.* **Performance:** *Maximum speed, 348 m.p.h. at 17,700 ft.; economical cruising speed, 280 m.p.h. at 18,700 ft.; maximum range, 4,475 mls.; maximum ceiling, 43,960 ft.* **Weights:** *Empty equipped, 49,384 lb.; maximum loaded, 97,885 lb.* **Dimensions:** *Span, 131 ft. 2¾ in.; length, 69 ft. 11⅓ in.; height, 18 ft. 4⅛ in.; wing area, 1,431.5 sq. ft.*

eliminating the forward gondola that had characterised all previous models of both the He 177 and 277, and overall length increased to 74 ft. 7¾ in., while the He 277B-6/R3 embodied still further fuselage redesign, the nose contours being finalised after the examination of more than 30 different nose mock-ups. The forward fuselage of the He 277B-6/R3 was somewhat deeper than that of the R2, and defensive armament included a similar manned FDL 151Z ventral gun position with twin 20-mm. cannon and a similar pair of weapons in the manned dorsal turret over the wing trailing edge. An FDL 131V "chin" barbette with four 13-mm. machine guns supplanted the FDL 131Z with twin weapons, and the remotely-controlled forward dorsal twin-cannon FDL 151Z barbette and HL/131V tail turret were retained.

The He 277B-7 was a long-range recon-naissance model derived from the He 177A-7 and featuring extended outer wing panels increasing overall span to 118 ft. 1⅛ in., and intended to take Jumo 213A, 213E or 222 engines with equal facility, but only one example was actually completed and this with DB 603A engines. The sole He 277B-7 was destroyed shortly before the arrival of Soviet troops.

HENSCHEL HS 123   GERMANY

Among the most important of the new weapons forged to aid the rebirth of German military power with the creation of the Third Reich was the *Sturzkampfflugzeug*—the dive bomber. Desultory interest in the potentialities of this type of warplane had been evinced in Germany from the earliest days of the embryo *Luft-waffe*, but it was the ardent support for the dive-bomber from the internationally-famous pilot Ernst Udet that led, in 1933, to an official specification for such a combat aircraft being drawn up, and it was under his aegis that the dive-bomber was subsequently developed.

In 1932, Gerhard Fieseler, the well-known aerobatic pilot, had acquired control of the Kegel-Flugzeugbau at Kassel-Bettenhausen, re-naming the company Fieseler Flugzeugbau, and with Udet's encouragement, the company initiated the design of an aircraft intended to fulfil the dive-bomber specification. Competing with the Fieseler concern to meet the requirements of the specification was the Henschel Flugzeugwerke which was estab-lished in 1933 by the Henschel und Sohn concern, manufacturers of locomotives and heavy road vehicles. Both companies de-signed clean, single-seat biplanes with metal monocoque fuselages, but whereas the Fieseler design, the Fi 98, was traditional in concept, being a two-bay aeroplane with a profusion of drag-evoking N-struts and bracing wires, its less elegant Henschel com-petitor, the Hs 123, was a single-bay sesqui-plane virtually devoid of wire bracing and having only two inclined aerofoil-section interplane struts.

Both Fieseler and Henschel completed their first prototypes during the early months of 1935, and although both aircraft employed the same 650 h.p. BMW 132A-3 nine-cylinder radial air-cooled engine, the latter company's dive bomber immediately evinced a marked performance ascendancy over the Fi 98, and it was a foregone conclusion from the earliest flight trials which aircraft would be the recipient of the production contract. The first Henschel prototype, the **Hs 123 V1**, made its

public début at Johannisthal, near Berlin, on May 8, 1935, three days after the existence of the *Luftwaffe* had been officially proclaimed, its pilot being Ernst Udet himself, his demonstration doing much to strengthen official interest in the *Sturzkampfflugzeug* which had been on the wane since the abortive testing of the Heinkel He 50A.

The first prototype was followed during the early summer months by two further prototypes, the **Hs 123 V2** (D-ILUA) and **V3** (D-IKOU), both having the original smooth NACA-type engine cowling supplanted by a shorter-chord cowling of reduced diameter which featured 18 small blisters enclosing the valve gear. The Hs 123 V3 also differed from its two predecessors in having the three-blade adjustable-pitch airscrew replaced by a two-bladed Hamilton Standard variable-pitch airscrew, and was the first prototype to carry armament—a pair of 7.9-mm. MG 17 machine guns fixed to fire forward through the engine cowling from the upper decking of the forward fuselage.

The trio of prototypes was quickly transferred to the *Erprobungsstelle* at Rechlin for official trials, but within three weeks of their arrival at Rechlin two had failed to recover from terminal velocity dives, the aircraft breaking up in the air and their pilots losing their lives. Analysis of the wreckage of the second specimen to crash revealed some considerable distortion of the upper wing centre section structure, leading to the surmise that this had resulted from the stresses exerted during the pull-out, the distorted members ripping out the struts carrying the centre section above the fuselage and leading to a progressive failure of the entire wing. Carefully controlled tests with the surviving prototype confirmed this conjecture, and the necessary wing centre section strengthening was incorporated in the newly-completed production prototype, the **Hs 123 V4** (D-IZXY).

The Hs 123 V4 reached Rechlin during the late summer of 1935, and apart from the beefing up of the wing centre section, incorporated

173

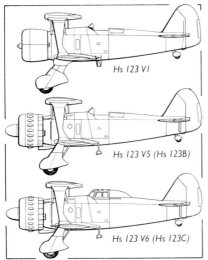

Hs 123 V1

Hs 123 V5 (Hs 123B)

Hs 123 V6 (Hs 123C)

a number of detail modifications intended to simplify production, including the replacement of the tailplane bracing wires by cantilever struts. Concentrated trials at Rechlin confirmed the effectiveness of structural modifications incorporated as a result of the earlier crashes, the aircraft being put through a series of dives at angles exceeding 80° from various altitudes, pull-outs offering no difficulties, and immediate production was ordered at Henschel's Schönefeld and Johannisthal factories.

Delivery of the **Hs 123A-1** to the *Luftwaffe* began during the summer of 1936, the production model differing from the V4 primarily

in having a BMW 132Dc direct fuel injection engine rated at 880 h.p. for take-off and 870 h.p. at 8,200 ft. The upper wing was a two-spar structure supported above the fuselage by N-struts, featuring metal skinning to the forward spar and fabric covering aft, and carrying the metal-framed, fabric-covered ailerons, the single-spar lower wing carrying the landing flaps. The fuselage was an oval metal monocoque, the fuel tank being housed immediately aft of the engine firewall, and the metal-framed tail surfaces having light alloy-covered fixed surfaces and fabric-covered movable surfaces. Built-in armament comprised two 7.9-mm. MG 17 machine guns, and the offensive load comprised a single 551-lb. bomb on a crutch between the undercarriage legs (although in service this crutch was normally used for an auxiliary tank) and underwing racks for four 110-lb. bombs.

The *Luftwaffe*'s first dive-bomber unit, the *Fliegergruppe* Schwerin, had been activated on October 1, 1935, this duly providing the nucleus for *Stukagruppe* I/162 "Immelmann" which initially operated a motley collection of Arado Ar 65s and Heinkel He 50s pending the availability of more suitable equipment. By the late autumn, by which time two further *Stukagruppen*, St.Gr.II/162 and I/165, had been formed, the Hs 123A had attained service with St.Gr.I/162, but civil war had now begun in Spain and the Condor Legion had been hurriedly organised to provide the Nationalist forces with air support, presenting an excellent opportunity to evaluate the efficacy of the *Luftwaffe*'s theories on dive-bombing in general and the Hs 123A in particular under combat conditions. *Oberst* Wolfram von Richthofen, the Legion's Chief-of-Staff, promptly requested the supply of a number of Hs 123A dive-bombers for evaluation, and five aircraft of this type reached Seville in December 1936.

174

(*Above*) *The Hs 123 V2, and (right) the Hs 123 V3*

Von Richthofen was more interested in the Hs 123A's potentialities as a *Schlachtflugzeug*, or close-support aircraft, however, than in its intended role of dive-bombing, and from their operational début early in 1937 the quintet operated primarily as a *Schlachtflieger* unit, testing his theories in the field. At that time, the principles of the Italian General Douhet prevailed more or less completely in the *Oberkommando der Luftwaffe* (OKL), little recognition being given to the possibility of aircraft taking a direct part in a land battle, the dive-bomber being regarded as chiefly a weapon for back area bombing. Despite co-operation with ground forces being of a most primitive kind, no ground-to-air R/T or even an effective method of signalling existing, the close-support operations of the Hs 123A were extraordinarily successful, the aircraft strafing and bombing with complete freedom directly over the battle zones. These pioneering efforts initially met with little response on the part of the OKL, although the Spanish Nationalists were sufficiently impressed to request the delivery of additional Hs 123As which were eventually supplied in the summer of 1938, 16 aircraft of this type, including those relinquished by the Condor Legion, forming the equipment of *Grupo* 24. The Hs 123A was dubbed the *Angelito* in Spanish service, and its sturdy construction and reliability endowed it with much popularity among Spanish crews. The 14 examples that survived the Civil War remained in first-line service in Spain for a number of years.

By April 1, 1937, when the decision was taken to double the *Stukagruppen* to a total of six, production deliveries of the Junkers Ju 87A-1 to St.G.162 (later redesignated St.G.2) had already commenced, and it was proposed that only two *Gruppen*, I/165 and the newly-activated II/165, would operate the Hs 123A, the remaining units receiving the more advanced Ju 87A. However, the importance of *Schlachtflieger* units as propounded by Wolfram von Richthofen finally impressed itself on the OKL which, on August 1, 1938, ordered the formation of five provisional *Gruppen* for close-support tasks.

The two Hs 123A-equipped *Stukagruppen* were now in process of converting to the Junkers Ju 87 (subsequently being redesignated I and II/St.G.77), and two of the five *Schlachtfliegergruppen*, SFG 10 and 50, were formed on the Hs 123As, the remaining three, SFG 20, 30 and 40, operating a mixture of Arado

(*Left*) *The production prototype, the Hs 123 V4*

176

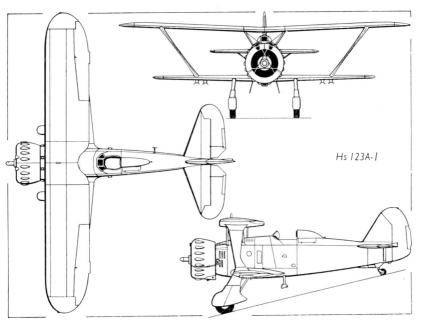

Hs 123A-1

Ar 66s, Heinkel He 46s and Heinkel He 51s. In the meantime, production of the Hs 123A was running out, Henschel's attempts to obtain production orders for improved versions of the basic design having been doomed to failure from the outset owing to the fact that the OKL was hypnotised by the apparent capabilities of the Ju 87 which, with good handling characteristics and manoeuvra-bility, and the ability to dive-bomb with an accuracy of less than 30 yards, seemed to possess ideal qualifications for a close-support aircraft. The decision was thus taken to re-equip all *Schlachtfliegergruppen* with the Ju 87, and in the autumn of 1938, production of the Hs 123A was finally phased out. The decision in fact amounted to a reverse for the protagonists of real close support, which term

was held to mean more or less direct and continuous participation in the land battle, as the Ju 87 was still considered primarily as a dive-bomber for pin-point attacks on targets behind the front line, and on November 1, 1938, after the Sudeten crisis had passed, the *Schlachtflieger* were disbanded.

Prior to the phasing out of Hs 123A production, two developments of the basic design had been built and tested, these being the **Hs 123 V5** and **V6**. The Hs 123 V5 (D-INRA) was intended as prototype for the proposed **Hs 123B** series, and differed from the production Hs 123A-1 in having a BMW 132K engine rated at 960 h.p. for take-off, driving a

(Left) An Hs 123A-1 (Werk-Nr. 968) of 2.J St.G 165 "Immelmann" (1937), and (below) an Hs 123A-1 in Spanish service

(Right) The Hs 123 V5, prototype for the proposed Hs 123B production series

three-blade variable-pitch airscrew and enclosed by an aerodynamically-refined, long-chord cowling. The Hs 123 V6 (D-IHDI), intended as a prototype for the **Hs 123C** series, was similar to its predecessor but intended specifically for the close-support role featured an additional pair of 7.9-mm. MG 17 machine guns which were mounted in the lower wings, an armoured headrest forming part of a raised streamlined fairing aft of the cockpit, and a sliding hood. The armoured headrest and aft fairing were shortly afterwards adopted as retrospective modifications for existing Hs 123A-1s.

With the disbanding of the *Schlachtflieger*, all aircraft were relegated to training and second-line duties with the exception of the Hs 123A-1s of SFG 10. This unit remained intact at Tutow and was incorporated into the newly-activated *Lehrgeschwader* 2 as II(*Schlacht*)/LG 2, and when, in September 1939, hostilities began in Europe, this was the *Luftwaffe*'s sole Hs 123-equipped close-support unit.

OPERATIONAL CAREER

During the latter half of August 1939, II(*Schlacht*)/LG 2 was transferred from Tutow to Alt Rosenburg, close to the Polish frontier. The *Gruppe* strength was 40 aircraft of which 37 were serviceable, and the unit formed a part of *Luftflotte* 4 on the southern flank. At first light on September 1, 1939, 36 Hs 123As of II(*Schlacht*)/LG 2 took-off on the first ground support mission of World War II. Throughout the Polish campaign, the Hs 123As concentrated on pinpoint attacks on Polish strongpoints and troop concentrations during which they proved particularly effective.

After 10 days' operations in Poland, the Hs 123A pilots discovered their most effective weapon to be not the twin MG 17 machine guns or the 110-lb. bombs but the psychological effect of the appalling noise emitted by the BMW 132 engine at certain revolutions. The optimum revs to achieve this noise, which sounded like heavy machine gun fire, was

179

1,800, although when the engine was running at such revolutions the synchronised machine guns could not be fired through fear of shattering the airscrew blades. Nevertheless, flying a few feet above enemy horse columns, the Hs 123As spread panic amongst both men and horses, and the columns dispersed in confusion.

The obsolescent Hs 123As achieved results that, measured by the number of bombs that they dropped or the rounds of ammunition that they fired, were quite astonishing and earlier plans calling for the re-equipment of II(*Schlacht*)/LG 2 were abandoned and the Henschel biplanes retained.

When, on May 10, 1940, the campaign in the West began, the unit was based at Laufenberg bei Neuss with 50 aircraft on strength of which 45 were serviceable, and forming part of von Richthofen's VIII *Fliegerkorps* under *Luftflotte* 2, this being the specialised close-support *Korps* charged with smashing a path across Belgium for the *Panzer* columns of von Reichenau's 6th Army.

On the first day of the campaign, II(*Schlacht*)/LG 2 constantly attacked Belgian troops endeavouring to blow bridges over the Albert Canal, and having helped to secure the crossings, the unit, together with the rest of VIII *Fliegerkorps*, was transferred to *Luftflotte* 3 to support *Panzergruppe* von Kleist's offensive through Luxembourg and the Ardennes. The Hs 123As co-operated with armoured columns in smashing two French divisions holding the Dyle positions on May 13th, subsequently participating in forcing the line of the Meuse and in the Battle of Sedan. Giving continual support to Guderian's XIX *Panzerkorps*, II(*Schlacht*)/LG 2 was transferred to Cambrai on May 21st, thus becoming the most forward *Luftwaffe* unit in France, and continued in action against pockets of French armoured resistance until the very end of the campaign.

This was also scheduled to be the end of the Hs 123A in first-line *Luftwaffe* service, and with the move of the VIII *Fliegerkorps* to Normandy for the forthcoming operations against the British Isles, II(*Schlacht*)/LG 2

(*Left*) *An Hs 123A-1 serving with Schlachtgeschwader 1 on the southern sector of the Russian Front in 1942*

A Henschel Hs 123A-1 of II (Schlacht)/LG 2 which performed the first ground support mission of World War II on September 1, 1939 from Alt Rosenburg

was withdrawn to Brunswick for conversion to the Messerschmitt Bf 109E and then sent to Böblingen for *Jabo* training. However, such had been the record of the Hs 123A during the French campaign—its remarkable ability to absorb enemy ground fire and sometimes direct hits from anti-aircraft shells and yet return to its base had become almost a legend in the *Luftwaffe*—that when II(*Schlacht*)/LG 2 moved South-East for the attack on the Balkans in April 1941, its equipment comprised a mixture of Bf 109Es and Hs 123As. The unit later transferred to the Eastern Front where it continued to operate until the turn of the year when the *Gruppe* was withdrawn for incorporation in the first of the newly-formed *Schlachtgeschwader*, this, Sch.G.1, being activated in January 1942 with the formation of two *Staffeln*, 1./Sch.G.1 at Werl and 8./Sch.G.1 at Lippstadt.

By the spring of 1942, 1./Sch.G.1 had provided the nucleus of a four-*Staffeln Gruppe*, becoming I/Sch.G.I, while the three *Staffeln* of the former II(*Schlacht*)/LG 2 had been redesignated 5., 6. and 7./Sch.G.1 to establish, with the existing 8.*Staffel*, the second *Gruppe*. By this time, 4./Sch.G.1 had completed working up on the Henschel Hs 129B-1, being transferred to the Eastern Front in May 1942, and thus the two *Gruppen* of *Schlachtgeschwader* 1 found themselves operating a mixture of Hs 123As, Bf 109Es and Hs 129Bs under *Luftflotte* 4 in the southern sector.

The now-elderly Henschel biplane quickly proved once more that true close-support was its real métier. Normally carrying four 110-lb. SC 50 bombs, two containers each of 92 4.4-lb. SC 2 anti-personnel bombs, or two 20-mm. MG FF cannon under the wings, the Hs 123A was continuously in the thick of the fighting.

181

(Left) An Hs 123A-1 sporting the "Infanterie-Sturmabzeichen", the close-support emblem, on the forward fuselage. Although it was proposed to phase out the Hs 123A early in W.W.II, it enjoyed such success in the ground support role that it lingered in first-line service until mid-1944

When the Bf 109Es and Hs 129Bs were grounded on the advanced airfields after rain had turned the runways into quagmires, the Hs 123As, with wheel cowlings removed, remained operational. Indeed, such was the value of this aircraft that, as late as January 16, 1943, General von Richthofen, commanding *Fliegerkorps Süd*, suggested in all seriousness to the *Reichsluftfahrtministerium* that the Hs 123A be reinstated in production. However, the proposal was impracticable as the jigs and tools had been scrapped in 1940.

In November 1942, I/Sch.G.2 joined operations, being followed by II/Sch.G.2 in January 1943, bringing to four the number of *Schlachtgruppen* on the Eastern Front. *Schlachtgeschwader* 1 continued to operate a diminishing number of Hs 123A biplanes until, in October 1943, the designation *Stukageschwader* was abandoned by the dive-bomber units, which had, in any case, converted mostly to close-support operations, and that of *Schlachtgeschwader* (now abbreviated as SG) adopted. The II/Sch.G.1, in which the Hs 123As were now concentrated, became II/SG 2 in the ensuing re-shuffle (I and III/SG 2 having previously been designated I and III/St.G.2 respectively). The Hs 123A continued in service with II/SG 2, combat attrition progressively reducing its numbers until, like the proverbial old soldier, it simply faded away, and by mid-1944 finally disappeared from the ranks of the *Schlachtflieger.*

HENSCHEL HS 123A-1
SPECIFICATION

Type: *Single-seat Dive-bomber and Close-Support Aircraft.* **Power Plant:** *One BMW 132Dc nine-cylinder radial air-cooled engine rated at 880 h.p. for take-off and 870 h.p. at 8,200 ft.* **Armament:** *Two 7.9-mm. MG 17 machine guns and (alternative) four 110-lb. SC 50 bombs, two containers of 92 4.4-lb. SC 2 anti-personnel bombs, or two 20-mm. MG FF cannon on underwing racks.* **Performance:** *Maximum speed, 212 m.p.h. at 3,940 ft., 207 m.p.h. at sea level; maximum cruising speed, 197 m.p.h. at 6,560 ft.; maximum range, 534 mls.; initial climb rate, 2,950 ft./min.; service ceiling, 29,525 ft.* **Weights:** *Empty, 3,316 lb.; normal loaded, 4,888 lb.* **Dimensions:** *Span, (upper wing) 34 ft. 5⅛ in., (lower wing) 26 ft. 3 in.; length, 27 ft. 4 in.; height, 10 ft. 6⅓ in.; wing area, 267.483 sq. ft.*

HENSCHEL HS 126   GERMANY

Until the early 'thirties, the short-range reconnaissance and army co-operation elements of most of the world's air arms were equipped with obsolescent aircraft generally designed for roles far removed from that of observing terrestrial activity. A growing appreciation of the importance of aerial tactical reconnaissance in modern warfare, however, led to a demand for aircraft designed specifically for co-operation with ground forces. The result was the design of a bevy of aircraft specifically for short-range reconnaissance and army co-operation for which

(Right and below) The Hs 126 V1 was an adaptation of the fourth Hs 122A-0 airframe and flew in the autumn of 1936

the classic single-engined high-wing monoplane formula was adopted almost universally.

It was considered unlikely that such aircraft would be called upon to operate for protracted periods in a hostile environment, the

(*Above*) *The Hs 126 V2 and* (*left*) *the Hs 126 V3, the latter having redesigned vertical tail surfaces and modified undercarriage*

accepted belief being that the army co-operation aircraft would rarely penetrate far into enemy-held territory without fighter cover, and would normally be within easy reach of its own lines. The essential features of such aircraft were held to be: the best possible view in all directions for the crew; the ability to take-off from and alight on small temporary landing fields or strips; ease of handling and good stability at low speeds to enable the pilot to concentrate on his task of observation, and an engine of sufficient power to enable the aircraft to get to and from the scene of operations relatively quickly.

As elsewhere, these conclusions were reached almost simultaneously in Germany and Britain, resulting in the appearance in 1936 of the Henschel Hs 126 in the former country and the Westland Lysander in the latter; aircraft of essentially similar concept and performance, although the British contribution to the state of the art was somewhat more sophisticated in the high-lift devices that it employed.

The Hs 126, which, by the beginning of World War II, equipped the bulk of the *Luftwaffe*'s *Aufklärungsstaffeln (H)* as a successor to the Heinkel He 46, was, in fact, evolved from an earlier design, the Hs 122, which had fallen short of its anticipated performance and had failed to offer a sufficient

advance over the He 46 to warrant quantity production. Powered by a liquid-cooled Rolls-Royce Kestrel engine, the **Hs 122 V1** (D-UBYN) had flown in the summer of 1935, being followed by the **Hs 122 V2** (D-UDIZ) and **V3** (D-UBAV) powered by the Siemens SAM 22B nine-cylinder air-cooled radial rated at 660 h.p. for take-off. A few Siemens-engined pre-production **Hs 122A-0** aircraft were completed by the Henschel Flugzeug-werke at Berlin-Johannisthal during the winter of 1935–36, but a major redesign of the aircraft was already under way. Embodying a revised wing, cantilever main undercarriage legs, a semi-enclosed cockpit and a more

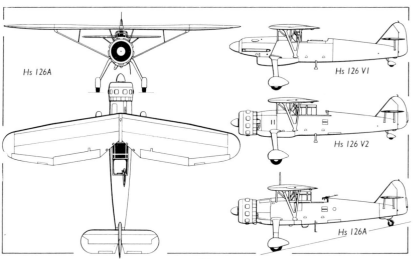

Hs 126A

Hs 126 V1

Hs 126 V2

Hs 126A

The Hs 126 V1 was employed for the investigation of basic handling characteristics and was joined in the test programme in the spring of 1937 by two additional prototypes, the **Hs 126 V2** (D-UJER) and the **Hs 126 V3** (D-OECY), both of which were powered by the Bramo 323A-1, the V2 featuring an exhaust-driven supercharger housed in a deepened portion of the forward fuselage. Apart from its power plant, the V2 differed from its predecessor in having a redesigned and enlarged rudder and an additional pair of tailplane bracing struts, while the V3 embodied still further redesign of the vertical surfaces. An additional change embodied by the Hs 126 V3 was to be found in the main undercarriage members. While the cantilever main legs of both the V1 and V2 featured a marked aft slope, those of the V3 were mounted at right angles to the fuselage centre line, the latter arrangement being adopted as standard.

Testing and evaluation of the Hs 126 V2 and V3 continued throughout the summer months of 1937, the aircraft fully meeting the *Luftwaffe*'s requirements, possessing pleasant

powerful engine, this aircraft, actually a conversion of the fourth Hs 122A-0 airframe, emerged in the autumn of 1936 as the **Hs 126 V1**.

Flown initially without the transparent sliding cockpit canopy, the Hs 126 V1 was powered by a 12-cylinder liquid-cooled Junkers Jumo 210 engine of 600 h.p. pending availability of the proposed Bramo Fafnir 323A-1 nine-cylinder radial air-cooled engine rated at 830 h.p. at 13,120 ft. and driving a three-bladed VDM variable-pitch airscrew.

somewhat staid handling characteristics, behaving docilely at the stall, and offering exceptional short-field performance. The spacious fuselage permitted the stowage of a considerable amount of equipment, the structure was exceptionally sturdy, and the structural design placed emphasis on ease of manufacture. While the flight testing of the prototypes was proceeding, Henschel began construction of a pre-production batch of 10 Bramo Fafnir 323A-powered **Hs 126A-0** aircraft, all of which had been completed before the end of 1937, several having been delivered for service evaluation to the *Aufklärungs-staffeln* (H), and these were followed on the assembly line by the **Hs 126A-1** which began rolling from Henschel's Schönefeld and Johannisthal facilities at the beginning of 1938, the first deliveries to the *Luftwaffe* commencing in the spring.

For reasons of availability, the Hs 126-A1 switched to the BMW 132Dc nine-cylinder radial air-cooled engine with direct fuel

injection rated at 880 h.p. for take-off and 870 h.p. at 8,200 ft. and driving a VDM control-lable-pitch airscrew. Stressed-skin construction was employed throughout. The two-spar wing was built in two halves joined on the centreline and carried above the fuselage by slightly-splayed steel-tube N-type cabane struts attached to the upper longerons, in-clined V-struts bracing the wings to the bottom of the fuselage, the struts themselves being rigidly braced to the rear spar by inverted V-struts at their mid-points. The wing trailing edges carried metal-framed, fabric-covered slotted ailerons and hydraulically-operated camber-changing flaps, the latter extending from the ailerons to the cut-out in the centre section.

The oval-section monocoque fuselage, which terminated at its forward end in four main longerons carrying the strut attachment points, engine bearers and main undercarriage members, accommodated the pilot beneath the wing centre section cut-out with the

(Below) An Hs 126A-0 *undergoing service evaluation with the Aufklärungsstaffeln (H) in the spring of* 1938

observer-gunner immediately aft. Both pilot and observer were enclosed by a transparent sliding canopy, and the gunner was provided with deflector panels enabling him to operate his gun free of slipstream.

All fuel was accommodated by a 119 Imp. gal. capacity tank mounted in the lower half of the fuselage, ahead and below the pilot, and a bay was provided in the fuselage aft of the observer housing a single Zeiss Rb fully-automatic topographic camera, the bay being covered by a panel in the bottom of the fuselage, this panel being opened and closed by means of a lever in the observer's cockpit. A hand camera was attached to the port side of the cockpit.

For light bombing missions the aft bay could be utilized to house two containers each with five 22-lb. bombs, and this offensive load could be augmented by a special rack which, attached to the port side of the fuselage and braced to the wing and lower fuselage longeron by auxiliary struts, could carry a single 110-lb. bomb. Armament comprised a single fixed forward-firing 7.9-mm. MG 17 machine gun in the upper decking of the forward fuselage starboard side with 500 rounds, and a single MG 15 of similar calibre on a flexible Arado mounting in the rear cockpit with a total of 975 rounds in 13 twin drums.

By September 19, 1938, the OKL returns indicated that a total of 42 Hs 126A-0 and A-1 aircraft had entered service with the *Luftwaffe's Aufklärungsstaffeln (H)*, 35 of these being serviceable, and to gain operational experience with the type, six Hs 126As were despatched to Spain in the late autumn of 1938 to replace the *Kette* of Heinkel He 45 biplanes operated by the Condor Legion's A/88 reconnaissance element. Employed over Spain for both tactical reconnaissance and light bombing missions during the closing stages of the Civil War, the Hs 126As proved eminently successful,

the five survivors eventually being handed over to the Spanish government and subsequently serving for several years in Morocco with 4 *Patrulla* of the *Ejercito del Aire*. Early in 1939 16 Hs 126A-1 aircraft were ordered by the Greek government for service with the Royal Hellenic Air Force, these subsequently equipping the 3rd Army Co-operation Squadron.

Production tempo built up rapidly, and by September 2, 1939, a total of 275 Hs 126s was in service with the *Luftwaffe* of which 254 were serviceable, the type having virtually supplanted the obsolescent Heinkel He 45 and 46 in service with the *Aufklärungsstaffeln (H)* distributed among the four *Luftflotten*, only six of the 29 *Staffeln* remaining equipped with the older aircraft, although seven other *Staffeln* still included a few He 46s in their first-line strength.

By this time the Hs 126A-1 had been supplanted in production by the **Hs 126B-1** which differed primarily in having the BMW Bramo Fafnir 323A-1, A-2, Q-1 or Q-2 nine-cylinder radial with two-speed supercharger and direct fuel injection driving a VDM 9-11 29 or 67 three-blade variable-pitch airscrew. Whereas the 323A-1 and Q-1 were rated at 850 h.p. at 2,450 r.p.m. for take-off and emergency, the A-2 and Q-2 offered 900 h.p. at 2,500 r.p.m. The Bramo offered full rated power at 13,780 ft., which was a marked improvement over the BMW 132Dc, and the Hs 126B-1 possessed both a better short-field performance and a better altitude performance than the Hs 126A-1. It also introduced improved radio equipment, FuG 17 VH, making its appearance on the type as standard.

For the invasion of Poland, *Luftflotte* 1 in North-East Germany possessed nine Hs 126-equipped *Aufklärungsstaffeln (H)* comprising 1. and 2.(H)/10, 1.(H)/11 (which included three He 46s on strength), 1, 2 and 3.(H)/21, and

, 2 and 3.(H)/41 (the last-mentioned unit included two He 46s on strength). The Hs 126s were active throughout the Polish campaign, and in addition to tactical reconnaissance, army co-operation and artillery spotting tasks, undertook a certain amount of strafing and also light bombing missions with the auxiliary bomb rack on the fuselage port side. Lack of effective anti-aircraft fire and limited fighter opposition gave the Hs 126 an ideal environment in which to operate, and attrition in the *Aufklärungsstaffeln* (H) was relatively low. In addition to Hs 126 units attached to *Luftflotte* , similarly-equipped *Aufklärungsstaffeln* (H) of *Luftflotte* 4 were also engaged actively in the Polish Campaign, these comprising 1.(H)/14 (which included three He 46s on strength), 2 and 3.(H)/14 (the latter including three He 46s on strength), and 1.(H)/31.

Luftflotte 2 in North-West Germany included three Hs 126A-equipped *Staffeln* on its strength, 1, 2 and 3.(H)/12, while *Luftflotte* in Southern Germany had seven Hs 126 *Staffeln*; 1, 2, 3, 4 and 5.(H)/13 (the last two mentioned units each including three He 46s and three He 45s on strength respectively),

4.(H)/22 and 1.(H)/23. Several of these units were engaged on photographic sorties over the Maginot Line during the opening months of the war, and despite the Hs 126's limited defensive armament, only light losses were

The Hs 126B-1 (below) had supplanted the Hs 126A-1 in production by the beginning of W.W.II and was manufactured until 1941

suffered, and production was continued, a total of 137 aircraft of this type being delivered between September 1, 1939 and the end of the year. By the early months of 1940, losses to fighters over the Western Front had begun to increase, underlining the fact that the concept of the Hs 126A was rapidly becoming obsolescent, and with the decision to manufacture the Focke-Wulf Fw 189 in quantity in April 1940, Hs 126 production was progressively tapered off, some 368 being manufactured in 1940 and the final five production machines leaving the line early in January 1941.

In the meantime, virtually all the remaining He 45s and He 46s were replaced by Hs 126s of which 277 were serving with the Luftwaffe on May 11, 1940, 234 of these being serviceable, and the first examples of the Henschel's intended successor, the Fw 189, had been delivered to 9.(H)/LG 2, a training Staffel forming part of the Lehrdivision, which had five Fw 189s and five Hs 126s on strength. By the time the assault on the Soviet Union began on June 22, 1941, 4.(H)/12, 4.(H)/21, 2 and 4.(H)/23, and 2 and 4.(H)/31 had all converted from He 45s and 46s to Hs 126s, and with the

exception of 2.(H)/14, which was to be the sole Staffel to operate the Hs 126 in North Africa, all the Aufklärungsstaffeln (H) were transferred to the Russian Front with their Hs 126s, serving in this theatre until replacement by the Fw 189 A and other types from the spring of 1942.

From mid-1942, the Hs 126 was progressively phased out of the first-line units and relegated to non-operational tasks such as glider-towing, in which role they served with II and III Gruppen of the Luftlandegeschwader 1 (Air Landing Wing 1) as tugs for DFS 230 transport gliders. With the formation of the Störkampfstaffeln for nocturnal harassing in the autumn of 1942, a number of Hs 126 were pressed into service, crewed by volunteers from the ranks of the A/B-Schulen instructors among others, and the Henschels continued in this role after these Staffeln were gathered together by the spring of 1943 in Nachtschlachtgruppen. Two such Gruppen were based in the Balkans, these using Hs 126 among a variety of other obsolescent types, and the last wartime operational missions of the Henschel included anti-partisan sorties.

HENSCHEL HS 126B-1 SPECIFICATION

Type: *Two-seat Tactical Reconnaissance and Army Co-operation Aircraft.* **Power Plant:** *One BMW Bramo Fafnir 323A-1 or Q-1 nine-cylinder radial air-cooled engine rated at 850 h.p. for take-off and 830 h.p. at 13,120 ft.* **Armament:** *One fixed forward-firing 7.9-mm. MG 17 machine gun in forward fuselage with 500 rounds and one 7.9-mm. MG 15 machine gun on flexible mounting in rear cockpit with 975 rounds. (Offensive) Ten 22-lb. bombs in aft fuselage bay (as alternative to fixed camera installation) and (optional) one 110-lb. bomb on auxiliary rack on fuselage port side.* **Performance:** *Maximum speed, 193 m.p.h. at sea level, 221 m.p.h. at 9,840 ft., 217 m.p.h. at 13,120 ft., 208 m.p.h. at 19,680 ft.; range (full fuel, no reserves), 360 mls. at 168 m.p.h. at sea level, 416 mls. at 189 m.p.h. at 6,560 ft., 447 mls. at 208 m.p.h. at 13,780 ft.; endurance, 2 hr. 15 min.; climb to 2,000 ft., 3.5 min., to 13,130 ft., 7.2 min., to 19,680 ft., 12.7 min.; service ceiling, 27,000 ft.* **Weights:** *Empty, 4,480 lb.; maximum loaded, 7,209 lb.* **Dimensions:** *Span, 47 ft. 6¾ in.; length, 35 ft. 7 in.; height, 12 ft. 3½ in.; wing area, 340 14 sq. ft.*

INDEX TO AIRCRAFT TYPES

References in **bold type** indicate primary coverage of basic model, other references relating to the initial mention of an individual aircraft sub-type or variant.